W9-AYK-860

Quilting a Poem

ORIGINAL DESIGNS INSPIRED BY AMERICA'S MOST BELOVED POETS

By Frances Kite and Debra Rowden

Quilting a Poem

ORIGINAL DESIGNS INSPIRED BY AMERICA'S MOST BELOVED POETS

By Frances Kite and Debra Rowden

Quilting a Poem
Original Designs Inspired by America's Most Beloved Poets

By Frances Kite and Debra Rowden
Edited by Doug Worgul
Book design and production by Kelly Ludwig
Quilt Blocks stitched by Jean Stanclift
Photographs by Tim Janicke
Templates by Gary Embrey

Published by KANSAS CITY STAR BOOKS
1729 Grand Boulevard
Kansas City, Missouri 64108

All rights reserved.
Copyright © 2003 The Kansas City Star

No part of this book may be reproduced, stored in a retrieval system, or
transmitted in any form or by any means, electronic, mechanical,
photocopying, recording or otherwise, without the prior consent of the
publisher.

First edition

Library of Congress Control Number: 2003103519

ISBN: 0-9722739-9-9

Printed in the United States of America
By Walsworth Publishing Company

To order copies call StarInfo at 816-234-4636

For more information about this and other fine books from Kansas City Star
Books visit our Web site at www.kansascitystore.com or www.pickledish.com.

TABLE OF CONTENTS

INTRODUCTION

*P*oems are like quilts. Carefully selected words stitched together, making a line. Lines painstakingly sewed one to another, creating an image. Images pieced to form a whole — an experience you can wrap around yourself for comfort, hang on a wall for inspiration, or keep in a chest to discover and rediscover like a cherished memory.

This book celebrates the relationship between poetry and quilting that quilters have long known exists. The quilt blocks in these pages are interpretations of some of America's most beloved poems. Poems you'll recognize from when your grandmother recited them to you at bedtime, or when you were introduced to them in your high school or college literature class.

Poems you knew you'd never forget.

I said these blocks are "interpretations." Poetry is not journalism. Poems interpret rather than describe the world. In that spirit, these quilt blocks interpret the poems upon which they are based. Using color, shape, tone and implication they suggest the mood, feeling and meaning of these poems. These blocks are inspirations, not illustrations. And like the poems that inspired them, they're unforgettable.

Frances Kite and Deb Rowden created these delightful blocks. Kelly Ludwig designed the book. Working with these women has been a joy. Now the joy is yours.

Doug Worgul, Editor

Kansas City • April 2003

*A*s an artist, I find inspiration in many places. In the poems selected for this book I was inspired by the qualities of atmosphere and emotion, and by the places described — both real and imagined.

I express myself through design and leave the writing to the authors. It has been a profound pleasure to use my visual vocabulary to interpret these poems. I hope that quilters who read this book enjoy the freedom to re-interpret these designs based on their own experiences and ideas.

Frances Kite

Baldwin, Kansas • April 2003

*A*t a flea market in Texas last fall, I found a quirky, bright, roughly made quilt smattered with teacups. It was love at first sight. I bought it from a sweet-faced woman who told me, "Sometimes the quilts just come to you." My collaborator Frances reminded me of this one day as I was fussing over how to make a pattern work. "These blocks are for inspiration," she said, "They're a starting point, something quilters can start with, then make their own designs and have fun with them. They don't have to make them exactly like this."

In other words, our purpose in creating this book is help the quilts come to you. There are poems here filled with emotion and life to set the mood and evoke color choice. And we've given you lovely and lively designs to place and play with as you please. I hope the book inspires you, as it has inspired me.

Deb Rowden

Lawrence, Kansas • April 2003

*F*rances Kite was destined to be a designer. As a child, she was captivated by every art, craft, or sewing project her mother introduced to her. As an adult, she majored in design at the University of Kansas, graduating cum laude in 1978. During her studies, Frances became intrigued with the process of cloisonné enameling. For 25 years she has created exquisite cloisonné art "jewelry for the soul," for which she has developed a loyal following. She has won over 42 awards and has exhibited in national and international shows. Her most recent honor is the inclusion of her brooch, "Traveling the Edge," in the permanent collection of the Smithsonian Institution's Renwick Gallery.

Recently Frances has collaborated with Debra Rowden on creating innovative new quilt designs.

*D*ebra Gehlbach Rowden was raised in Lawrence and Shawnee, Kansas. Growing up she enjoyed playing with paper dolls, reading and sewing. In high school, she dreamed of becoming an artist. In college, she studied to become a journalist. Ever since, she's worked with both words and fabric. She earned a Bachelor of Science degree in Clothing & Textiles/Mass Communications from Kansas State University in 1977. She took her first quilt class the next year and hasn't stopped quilting since. She confesses to starting more quilts than she finishes. Deb collects primitive quilts, and meets weekly with a small, but raucous, quilt group in Lawrence, Kansas, where she lives with her husband, two daughters, two dogs and two cats. She considers Lawrence to be the hotbed of quilting and the center of the universe.

ACKNOWLEDGMENTS

Thanks first and foremost to the unflappable Jean Stanclift of Lawrence, Kansas who stitched the blocks for this book. We can't thank her enough. We also thank our independent quilt shops, Sarah's and Stitch-On Fabrics, for giving us choice and supporting local quilters.
— D.G.R. and F.K.

For Dwain, a never-ending source of inspiration and support.
— F.K.

Thanks to everyone who makes me laugh. Thanks to everyone who's inspired me. I've thought of you as I worked on this project. Thanks most of all to my dear family for surrounding me with love and good times.
— D.G.R.

Use the quilt methods you like most. We give instructions for machine stitching, but hand appliqué will work on most of these blocks.

Always wash your fabric before you begin. Some colors will bleed, as we all know.

All seams are 1/4 inch, unless otherwise specified.

Press pieced blocks open at every step, gently but firmly. As with all quilt blocks, seams are pressed toward the same direction, not opened up.

MACHINE APPLIQUÉ USING FREEZER PAPER

When I began looking at quilts, I admired the appliquéd quilts, quite sure I would never be skilled enough to make one. Happily, several years ago I took several classes and learned how to use freezer paper templates for appliqué and I've been appliquéing ever since. It's simple and accurate. You do glue as much as you stitch, though. This makes some quilters grumble.

How it works
Get a roll of **freezer paper** from your local grocery store. It is plastic coated. It only comes in huge amounts: one box will last you a long time. One side of the paper is dull, the other glossy. The shiny side will adhere to the backside of your fabric. The dull side is good for marking.

Examine your pattern pieces. If they face one direction or the other, you need to be careful when drawing your shapes. If you have a light box, place your pattern on it facing down. Then you can lay your freezer paper over it, glossy side down and trace the pattern piece and it will face the right direction. I don't have a light box so I tape my pattern on the window to trace. Use a pencil to trace your pieces

Cut out the paper pattern on the lines (don't leave a seam allowance on the paper). Fire up your iron, position the piece glossy side down where you want it on the backside of the fabric and iron. It will stick. You can even pick it up and move it and it will usually stick again if needed.

Cut out the fabric around the piece, leaving a seam allowance to turn. It should be scant, like 3/16″. Study your pattern to see what edges will show. Many of the blocks in this book have pieces layered on top of each other. You only need to glue under edges that will show.

Clip inside curves, like those shown on our feather pieces. Cut very close to but not into the paper.

Glue under the edges. Use enough glue to hold the fabric in place, but don't slather it on. I use water-soluble glue sticks from the kids school supplies section in the store. There is a fancy brand that others swear by. Work carefully so your edges are smooth. (You get better at this with practice.) I usually stow my glued pieces in a book so they stay glued. If you glue a long time before you stitch, they often come unglued.

Position the piece on the background where you want it. Stitch it in place. The best machines have a stitch setting that meanders gently along the ditch of the piece and occasionally catches the background (our stitcher Jean's does this). My machine only has a narrow zig-zag stitch--that works too. What's important is that the needle is positioned to fall just beside the outside of the paper piece: the rest of the stitching needs to catch the piece. We use the beautiful muted colors of DMC thread. I set my zig-zag stitch setting to be not too tight.

Trim. Once you've stitched all your pieces in place, turn the block over and trim the excess fabric from the background.

Then remove the paper. I squirt mine with water from a spray bottle, let it soften for a minute, then gently pull it away. If that doesn't work, wet a cloth and gently work the edge a bit to get the glue to loosen. For long, thin pieces, try using tweezers to pull the paper loose. On layered blocks, you will have to repeat this process until you have all the paper removed.

Once the block is dry, **press.**

PAPER PIECING

Many of our blocks feature small pieced areas. These are not difficult to recreate if you use paper piecing.

Paper piecing is foundation piecing. Use a paper pattern as your foundation. It stabilizes fabric so you can place it off-grain. It makes it easy to sew even our small shapes very accurately.

One caution: paper piecing does use more fabric than other piecing methods. The way you place the fabric generously to cover the necessary shape wastes some fabric. But if you like to make scrap quilts, you have leftover scraps.

How it works
Let's walk through the steps using the most difficult paper piecing block in the book first, the D/E/F/G/H block from *So Much Happiness*.

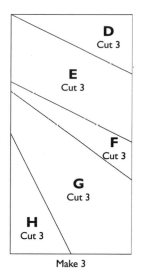

D
Cut 3

E
Cut 3

F
Cut 3

G
Cut 3

H
Cut 3

Make 3

- Next, cut a generous block of fabric for F. Place it against G, right sides together, making sure 1/4″ seam allowance extends beyond stitching line. Turn to the backside of the pattern and stitch. Use a slightly smaller stitch length than usual, but not so small that you can't rip out the stitches if needed. If you have to remove stitches, tape the paper back together if it comes apart.

- Trim seam allowance. Fold back everything but the seam allowances and trim seam allowance to 1/4 ″.

- Turn back to front side. Press.

- Repeat these steps to add Ɛ, then D, then H.

- Trace the pattern. Transfer all lines to the backside of the pattern too. Mark the front side of the pattern clearly. That is the side your fabric is placed on. Note: our block is the actual block size. When you trim, leave a 1/4 ″ seam allowance around the block.

- Study the block. This block has five pieced areas. It's best to start with the biggest piece, so we will piece G first.

- Place fabric on top of G, right side up. The fabric does not need to be cut to size now, just ample enough to cover the piece plus seam allowances on outer edge. Pin in place.

- Trim seam allowance around entire block to 1/4″.

- Leave the paper in place as you join the block with other blocks—it serves as a stitching guide and keeps the block stable.

- Once you are done, the paper will easily tear off the back. That's the fun part.

so much depends

upon

a red wheel

barrow

glazed with rain

water

beside the white

chickens.

William Carlos Williams
1883-1963

William Carlos Williams was the poet of the commonplace. His works used language spoken by real Americans in their everyday lives. His images were instantly recognizable and thoroughly accessible. In addition to achieving international success as a poet, novelist, playwright and essayist, Williams was also a practicing physician.

THE RED WHEELBARROW

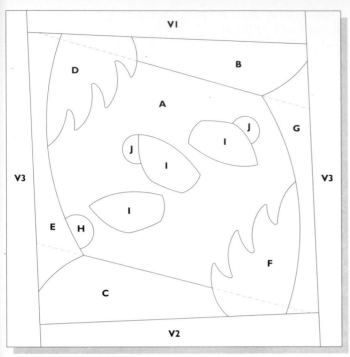

Finished block size: 14″ x 14″

Techniques: appliqué

Fabrics

Fat quarters (18″ x 22″)

- background
- red border
- gray border
- outer border

Scraps

- D, F feather
- I wheelbarrows
- H, J wheels

Directions

- Cut out background A and borders. Make freezer paper templates for B, C, D, E, F, G, H, I (3), and J (2) — fuse onto fabric. Cut pieces out and glue under edges that will show.
- Appliqué B and C to background A.
- Appliqué D and E + H, F and G.
- Add borders in this order: V1, V2, then V3s.
- Appliqué two J wheels and three I wheelbarrows.

Tips:

Study the pattern before you start. For many of these appliquéd pieces, you only need to glue under edges that will show.

- For C and B, only turn under one edge.
- Place D first, then layer E over it. Their outer edges do not need to be turned under. Follow the same steps for F, then G.

D
Cut 1

F
Cut 1

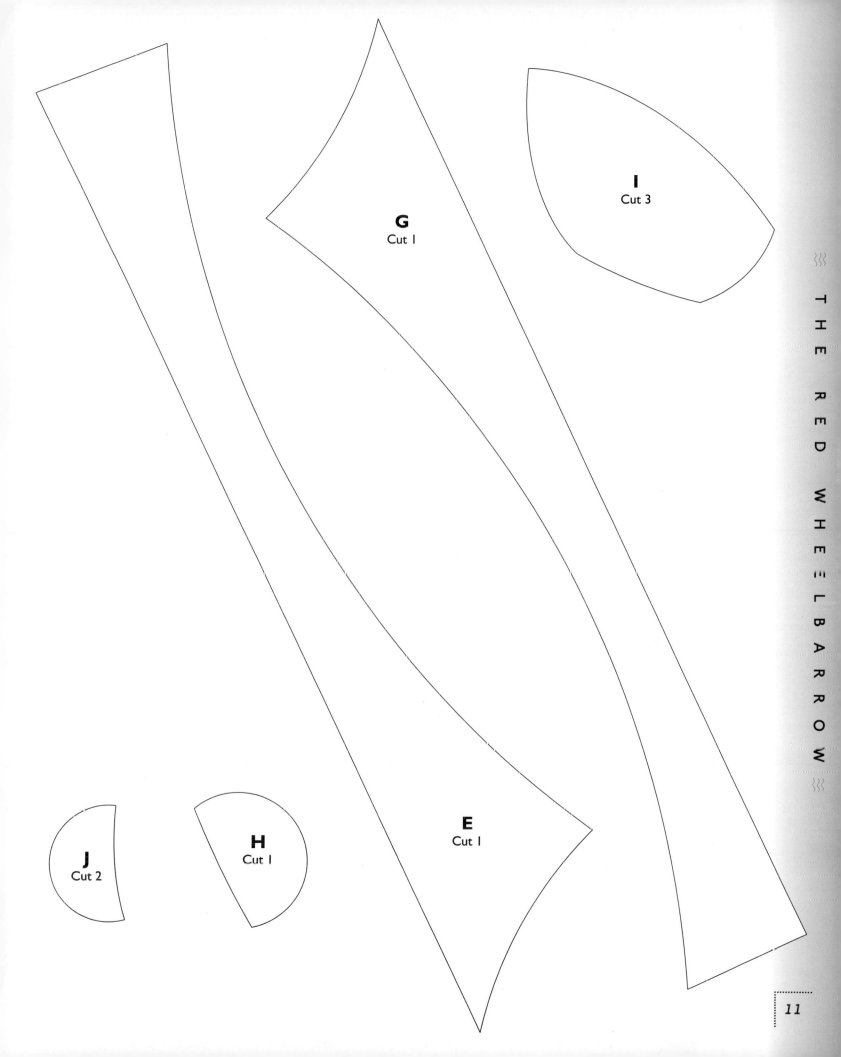

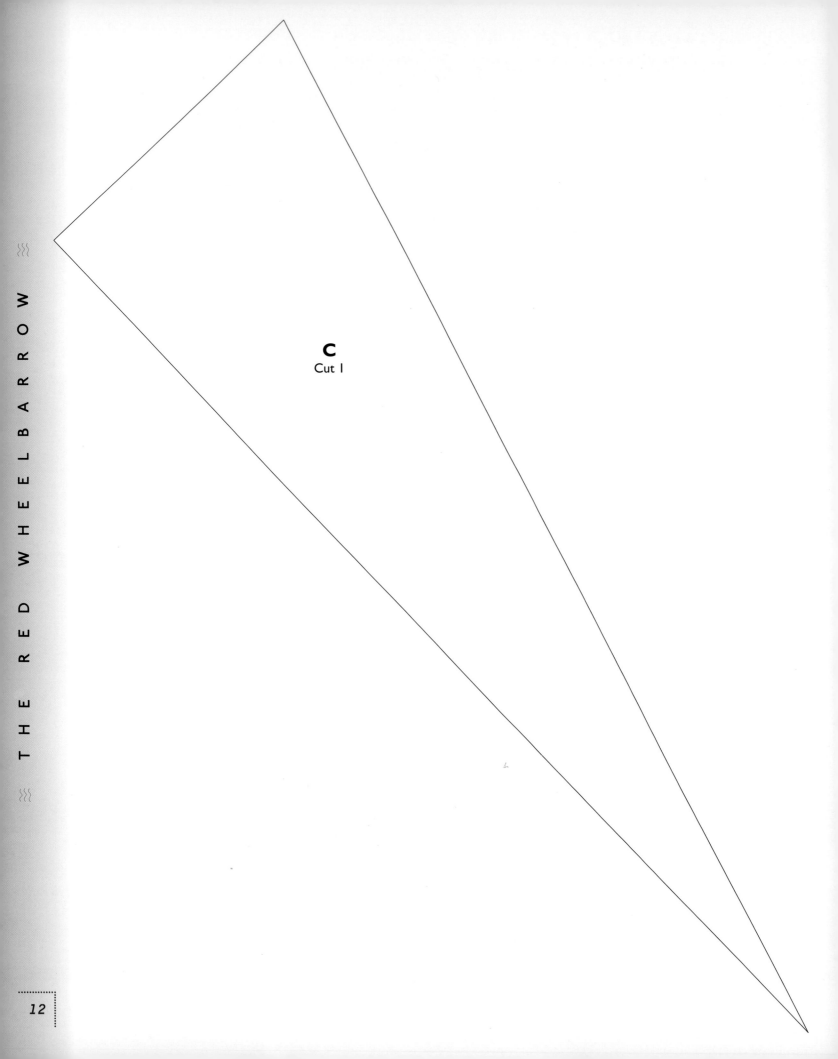

C
Cut 1

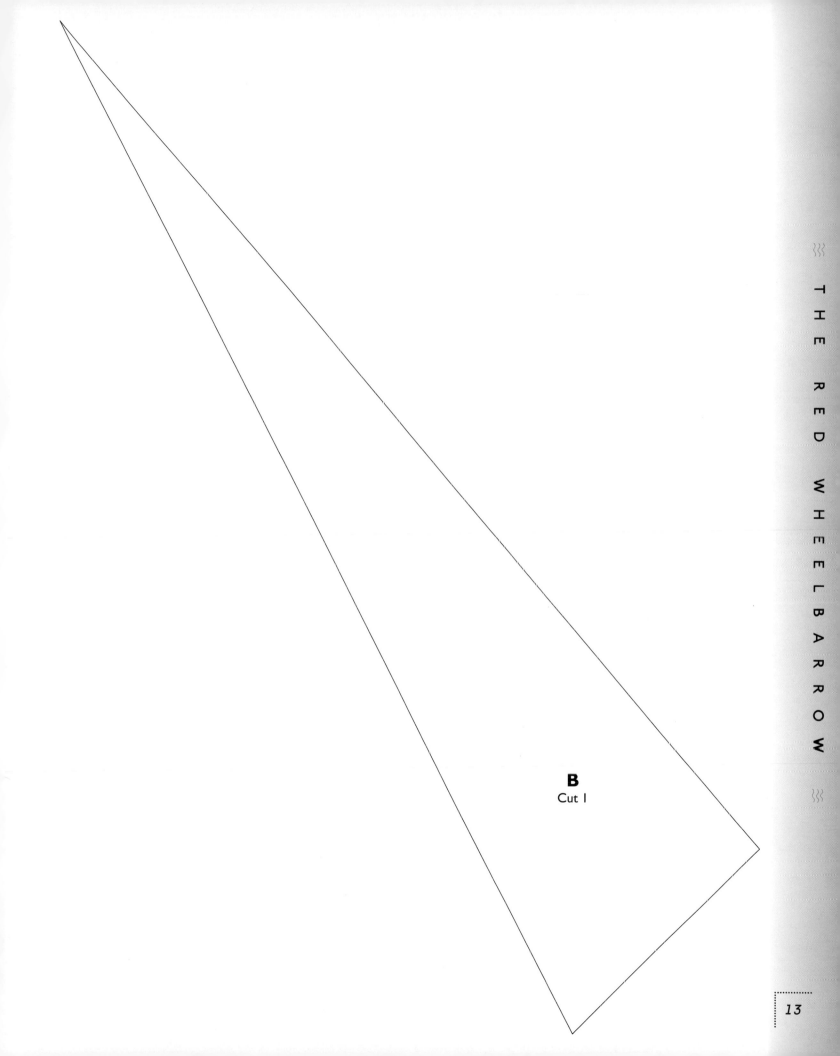

B
Cut 1

F E A S T
Edna St. Vincent Millay

I drank at every vine.

The last was like the first.

I came upon no wine

So wonderful as thirst.

I gnawed at every root.

I ate of every plant.

I came upon no fruit

So wonderful as want.

Feed the grape and bean

To the vintner and monger;

I will lie down lean

With my thirst and my hunger.

Edna St. Vincent Millay
1892–1950

In spite of a controversially Bohemian lifestyle, Edna St. Vincent Millay was an enormously popular and important poet during her lifetime. Her poems, which are at turns witty and biting and hauntingly beautiful, reduce the human experience to essential themes; longing, love, loss, need, greed, joy, despair and death.

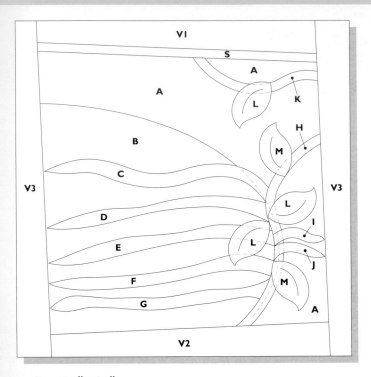

Size: 14″ x 14″

Techniques used: appliqué

Fabrics

Fat quarters (18″ x 22″)

- border
- grape
- background
- accent strip

Scraps

- greens

Directions

- Cut out background A and borders. Make freezer paper templates for B, C, D, E, F, G, H, I, J,K, L (3) and M (2) — fuse onto fabric. Cut pieces out and glue under edges that will show.
- Appliqué C, D, E, F and G to B.
- Appliqué B to A.
- Appliqué H and K.
- Appliqué leaves M (2) and L (3), I and J.
- Add accent strip S. A pattern piece is provided if you would like to piece or appliqué S. You can also try this: cut strip 1″ wide, 12 1/2″ long. Fold in half lengthwise, right sides out. Press. Follow pattern and position in place on right side of background, edges together. Glue in place.
- Add borders in this order: V1, V2, then V3s.

Tips:

If you use freezer paper appliqué for this block, have a pair of tweezers handy when it's time to remove the paper.

D
Cut 1

C
Cut 1

FEAST

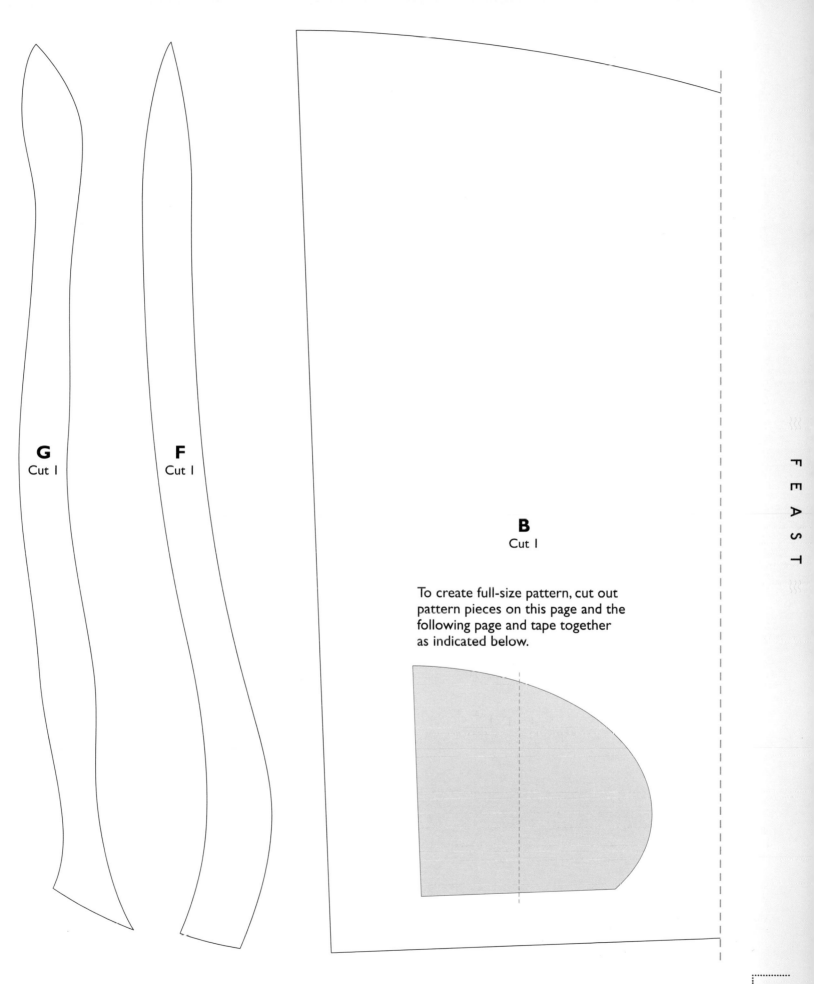

G
Cut 1

F
Cut 1

B
Cut 1

To create full-size pattern, cut out pattern pieces on this page and the following page and tape together as indicated below.

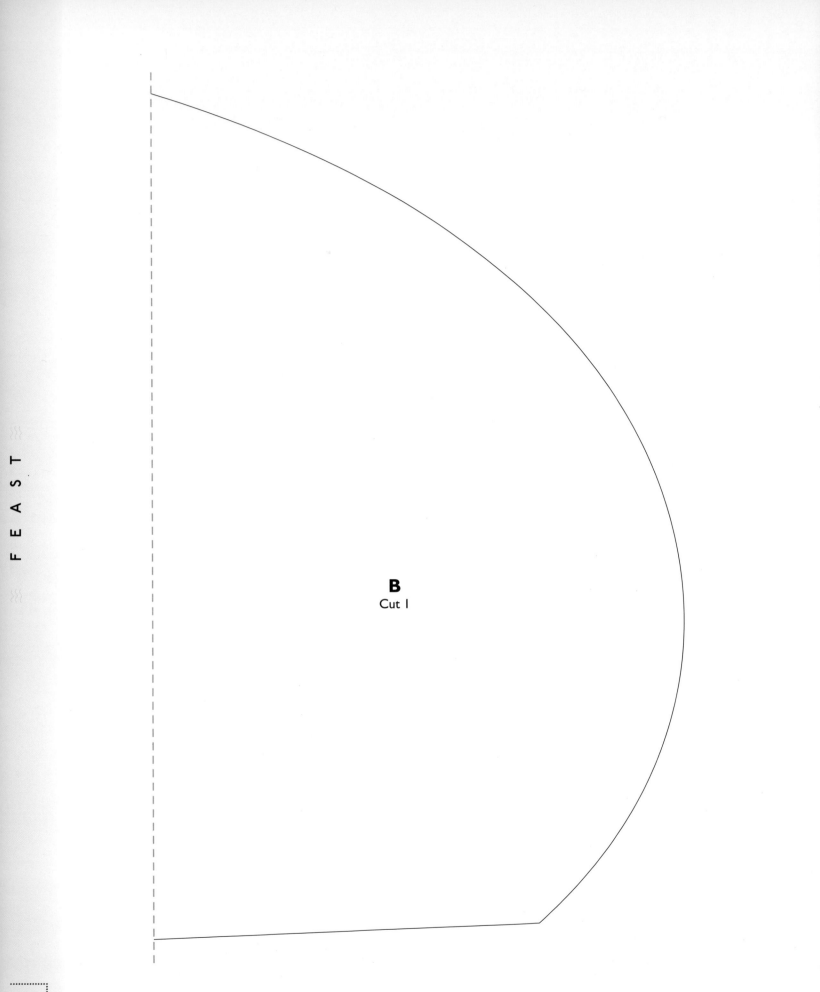

B
Cut 1

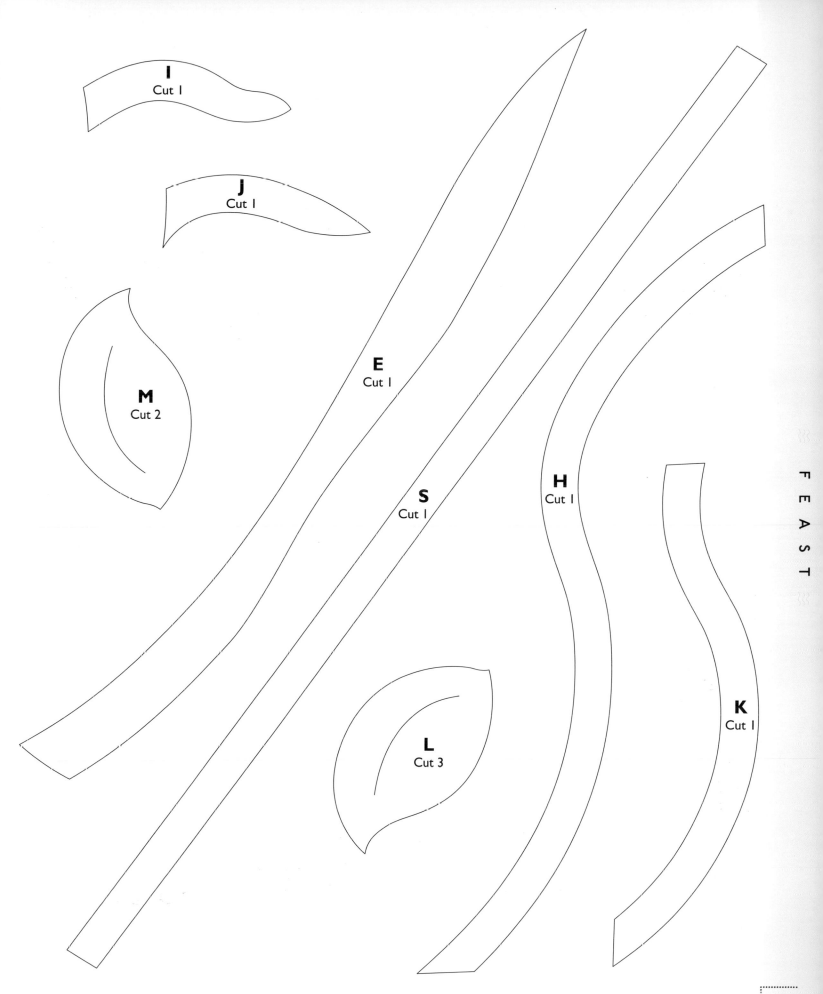

I have eaten
the plums
that were in
the icebox

and which
you were probably
saving
for breakfast

Forgive me
they were delicious
so sweet
and so cold

William Carlos Williams
1883-1963

Williams devotion to his patients and to his hometown of Rutherford, New Jersey, where he was born and where he practiced medicine, was a primary influence on his poetry. His work examined and celebrated the lives of working-class people. He received the Pulitzer Prize in 1963.

THIS IS JUST TO SAY

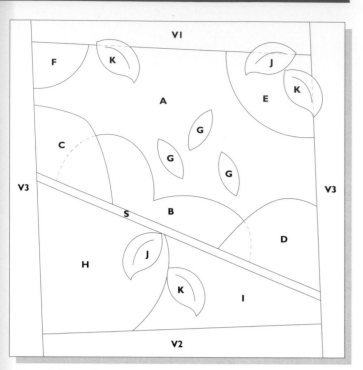

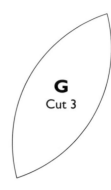

G
Cut 3

Size: 14″ x 14″

Techniques used: appliqué

Fabrics

Fat quarters (18″ x 22″)
- border

Scraps
- E, F, H, I plums
- B bowl
- C, D icebox
- leaf green
- G pits
- strip accent

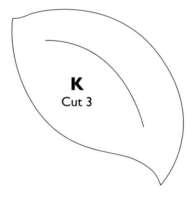

K
Cut 3

Directions

- Cut out background A and borders. Make freezer paper templates for B, C, D, E, F, G (3), H, I, J (2), and K (3) —fuse onto fabric. Cut pieces out and glue under edges that will show.
- Appliqué B, C, D, E and F to A.
- Appliqué H to I. Match edges to bottom of background A.
- Appliqué accent strip S.
- Add borders in this order: V1, V2, then V3s.
- Appliqué J/K leaves, and G pits.

Tips:

This is another block that has many applique edges that will not have to be turned under. The line on leaves K and J could be a quilted line or other stitched embellishment.

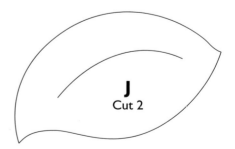

J
Cut 2

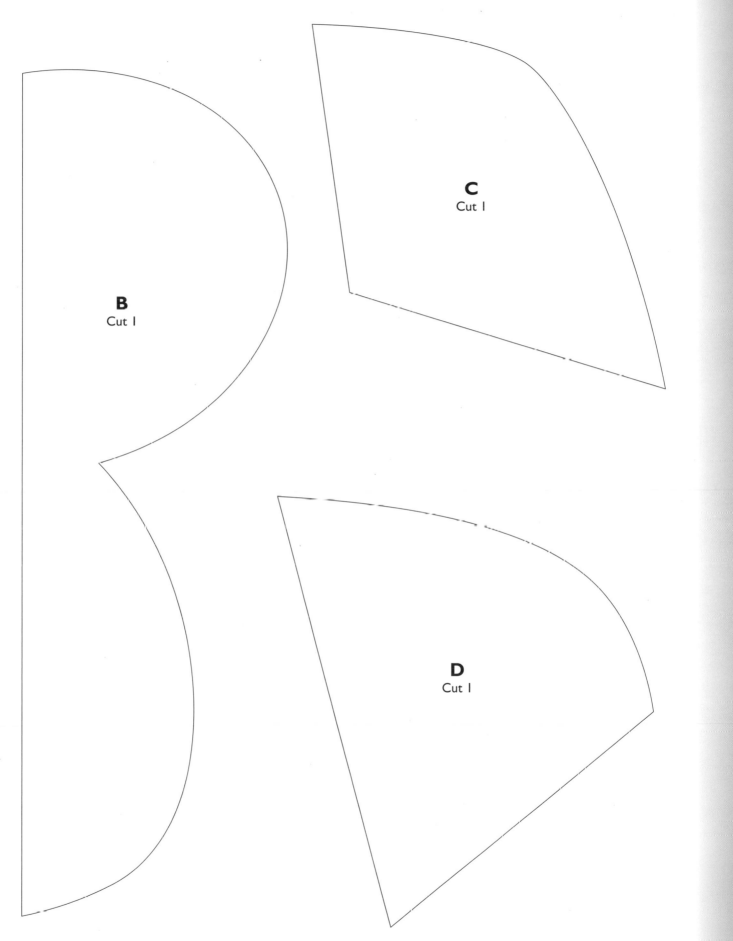

B
Cut 1

C
Cut 1

D
Cut 1

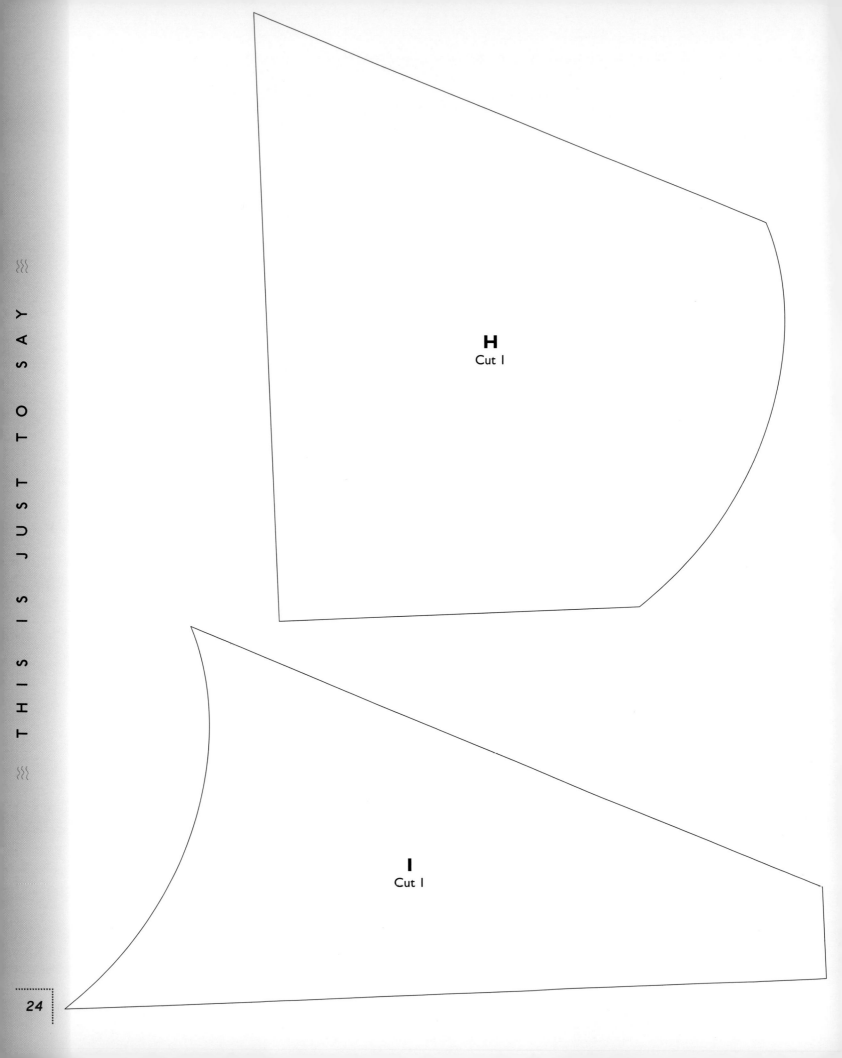

H
Cut 1

I
Cut 1

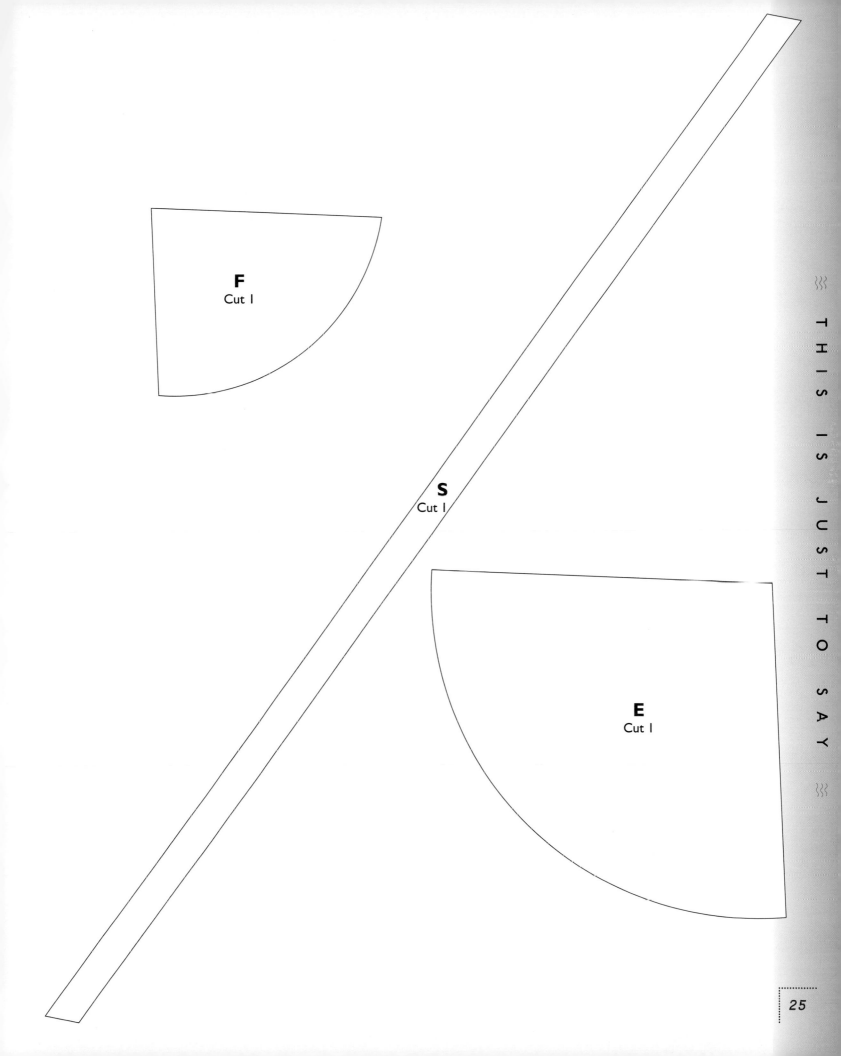

F
Cut 1

S
Cut 1

E
Cut 1

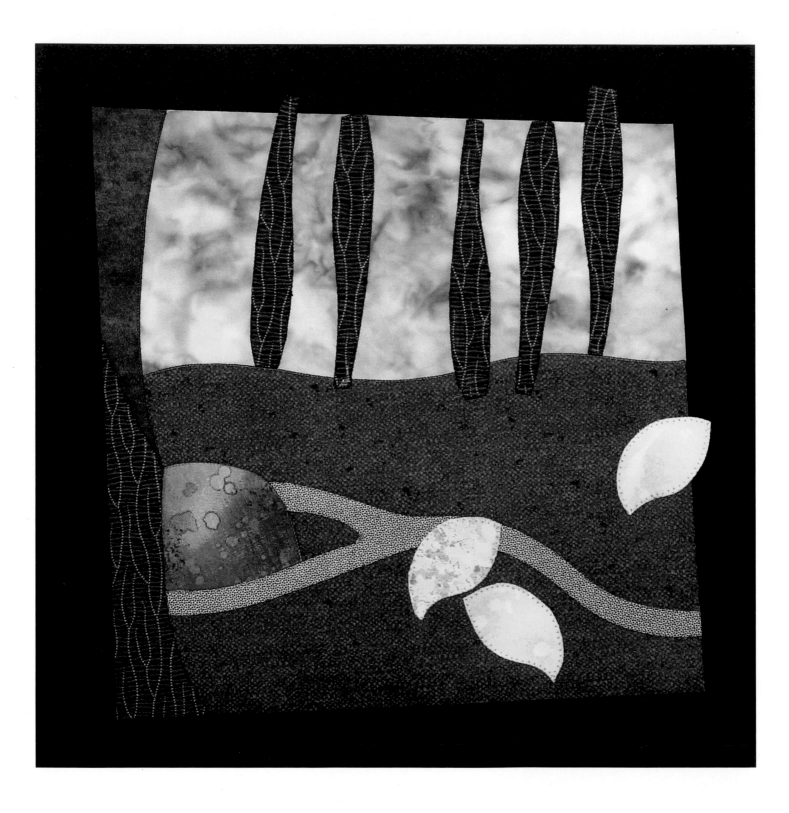

Two roads diverged in a yellow wood,

And sorry I could not travel both

And be one traveler, long I stood

And looked down one as far as I could

To where it bent in the undergrowth;

Then took the other, as just as fair,

And having perhaps the better claim,

Because it was grassy and wanted wear;

Though as for that the passing there

Had worn them really about the same,

And both that morning equally lay

In leaves no step had trodden black.

Oh, I kept the first for another day!

Yet knowing how way leads on to way,

I doubted if I should ever come back.

I shall be telling this with a sigh

Somewhere ages and ages hence:

Two roads diverged in a wood, and I—

I took the one less traveled by,

And that has made all the difference.

Robert Frost
1874-1963

Robert Frost is perhaps the most beloved, yet misunderstood, American poet of the Twentieth century. Upon first reading, most of Frost's poems seem to be about nature and man's relationship to the natural world. Repeated readings reveal darker, more complex psychological themes that speak to a universal human condition.

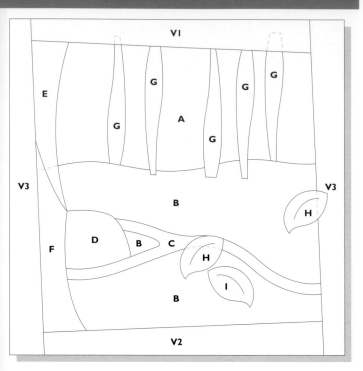

Finished block size: 14″ x 14″

Techniques: appliqué

Fabrics

Fat quarters (18″ x 22″)

- background A
- foreground B
- border

Scraps

- C road
- D rock
- E, F tree
- G trees
- H, I leaves

Directions

- Cut out background A and borders. Make freezer paper templates for B, C, D, E, F, G (5), H (2) and I—fuse onto fabric. Cut pieces out and glue under edges that will show.
- Appliqué B to A.
- Appliqué C and D.
- Appliqué E, F.
- Arrange G trees as shown, appliqué.
- Add borders. Stitch borders on in this order: V1, V2, then V3s.
- Appliqué two H and I leaves.

Tips:

Arrange G trees as shown or design your own woods - they could also extend onto outer border. Again, leaves can be embellished with quilting and stitching.

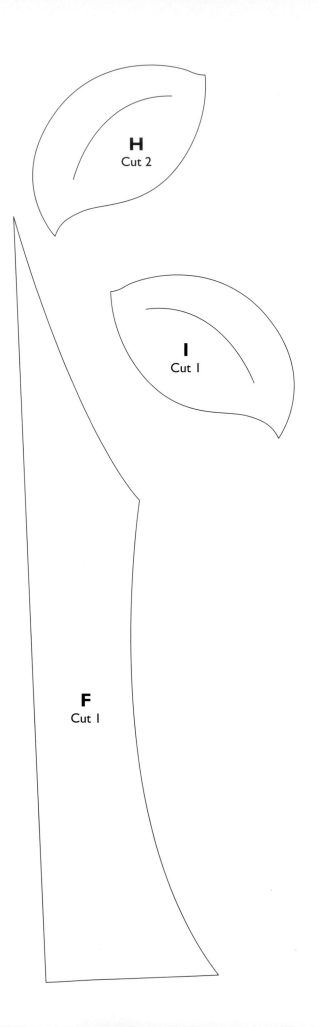

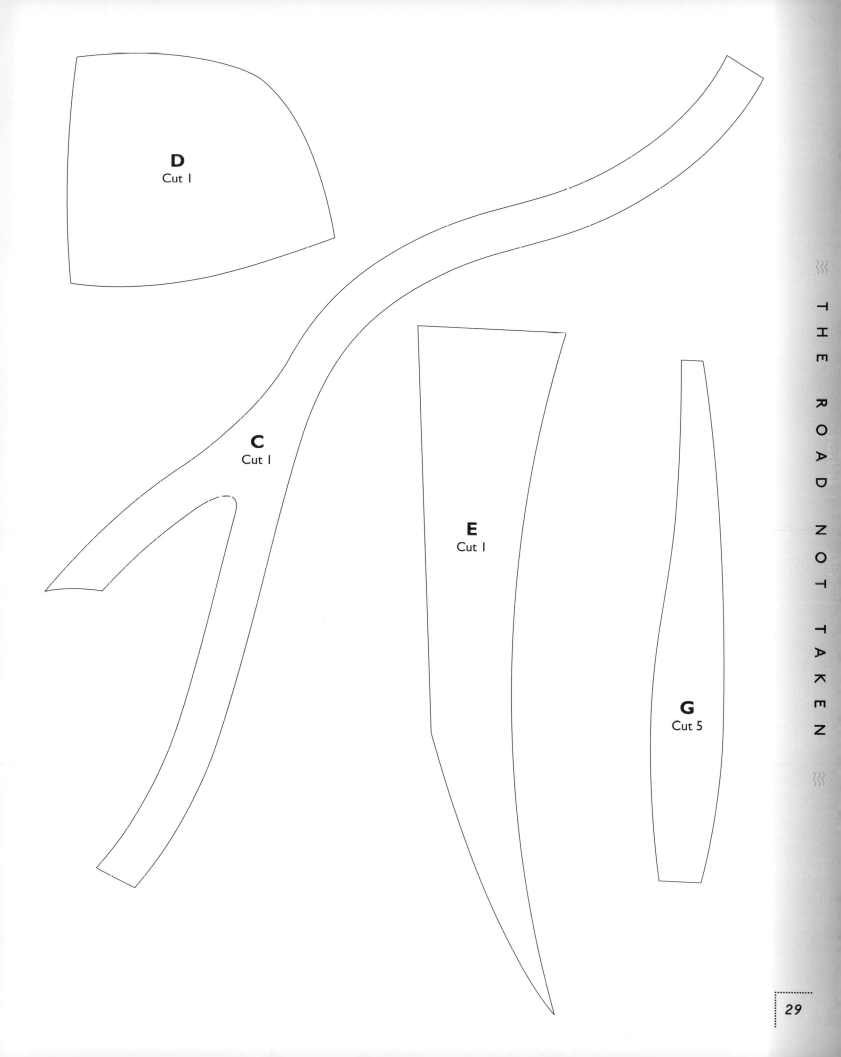

D
Cut 1

C
Cut 1

E
Cut 1

G
Cut 5

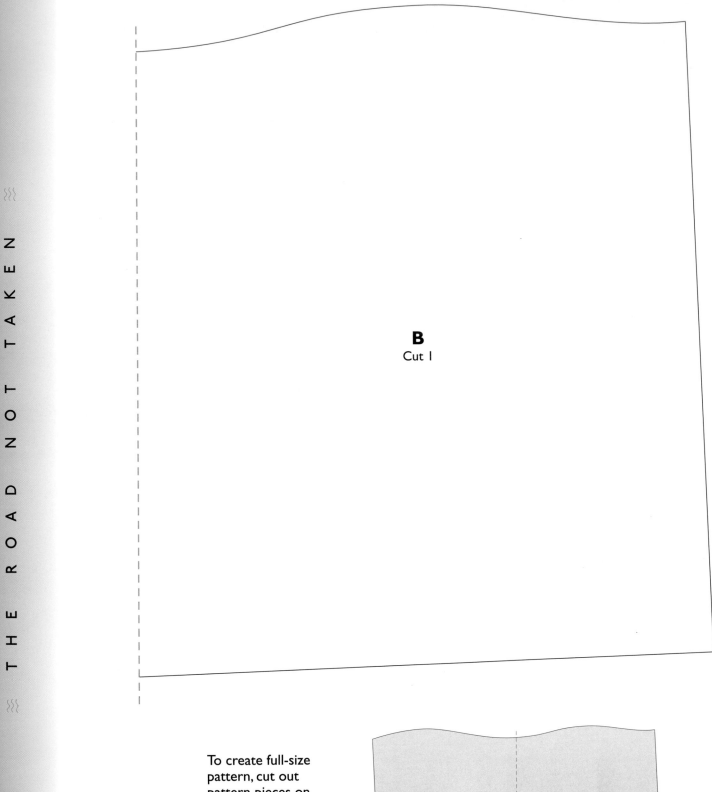

B
Cut 1

To create full-size
pattern, cut out
pattern pieces on
this page and the
following page
and tape together
as indicated
to the right.

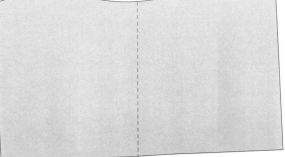

B
Cut 1

STOPPING BY WOODS ON A SNOWY EVENING

Robert Frost

Whose woods these are I think I know.

His house is in the village though;

He will not see me stopping here

To watch his woods fill up with snow.

My little horse must think it queer

To stop without a farmhouse near

Between the woods and frozen lake

The darkest evening of the year.

He gives his harness bells a shake

To ask if there is some mistake.

The only other sound's the sweep

Of easy wind and downy flake.

The woods are lovely, dark and deep.

But I have promises to keep,

And miles to go before I sleep,

And miles to go before I sleep.

Robert Frost
1874-1963

Although he is thoroughly and intimately associated with New England, Frost was actually born in San Francisco. He moved to Massachusetts when he was eleven years old. And though he attended both Dartmouth and Harvard and taught at colleges and universities, he never earned a college degree. He did, however, earn four Pulitzer Prizes.

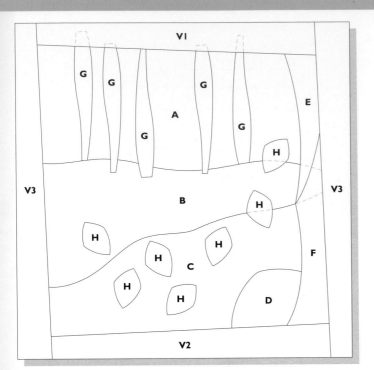

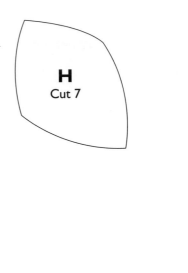

H
Cut 7

G
Cut 5

Finished block size: 14″ x 14″

Techniques: appliqué

Fabrics

Fat quarters (18″ x 22″)
- background
- foreground B
- foreground C
- border

Scraps
- E, F tree
- G trees
- D rock
- H snowflakes

Directions
- Cut out background A and borders. Make freezer paper templates for B, C, D, E, F, G (5), and H (7)—fuse onto fabric. Cut pieces out and glue under edges that will show.
- Position C and B on background A, appliqué.
- Appliqué D.
- Appliqué E, F.
- Arrange G trees as shown, appliqué.
- Add borders in this order: V1, V2, then V3s.
- Appliqué H snowflakes.

Tips:

The snowflakes could be embellished in many ways — use your imagination.

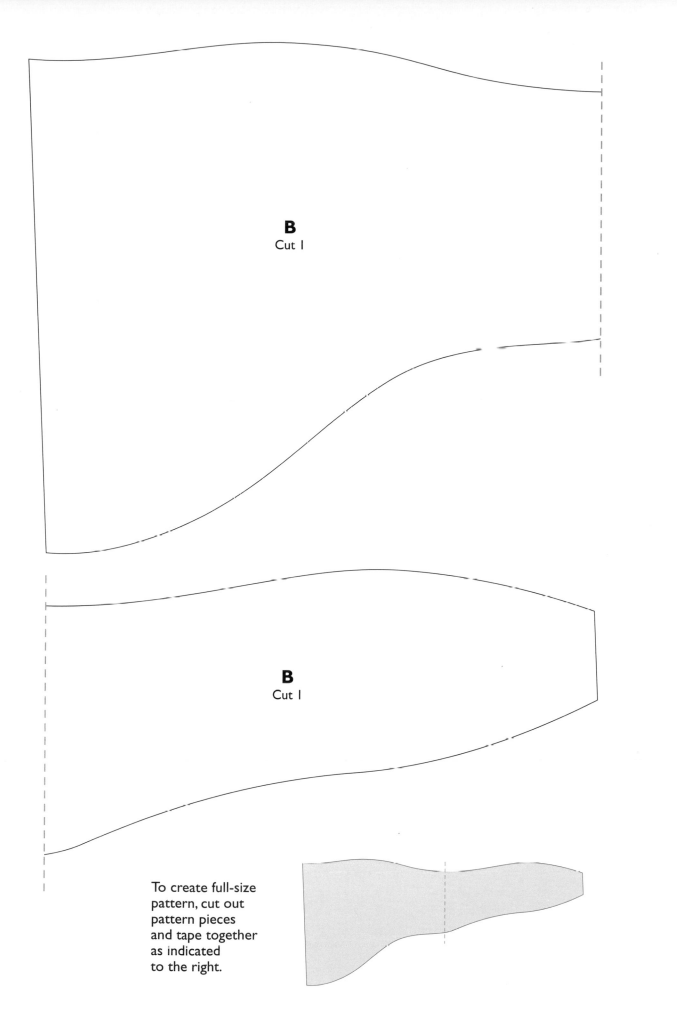

B
Cut 1

B
Cut 1

To create full-size
pattern, cut out
pattern pieces
and tape together
as indicated
to the right.

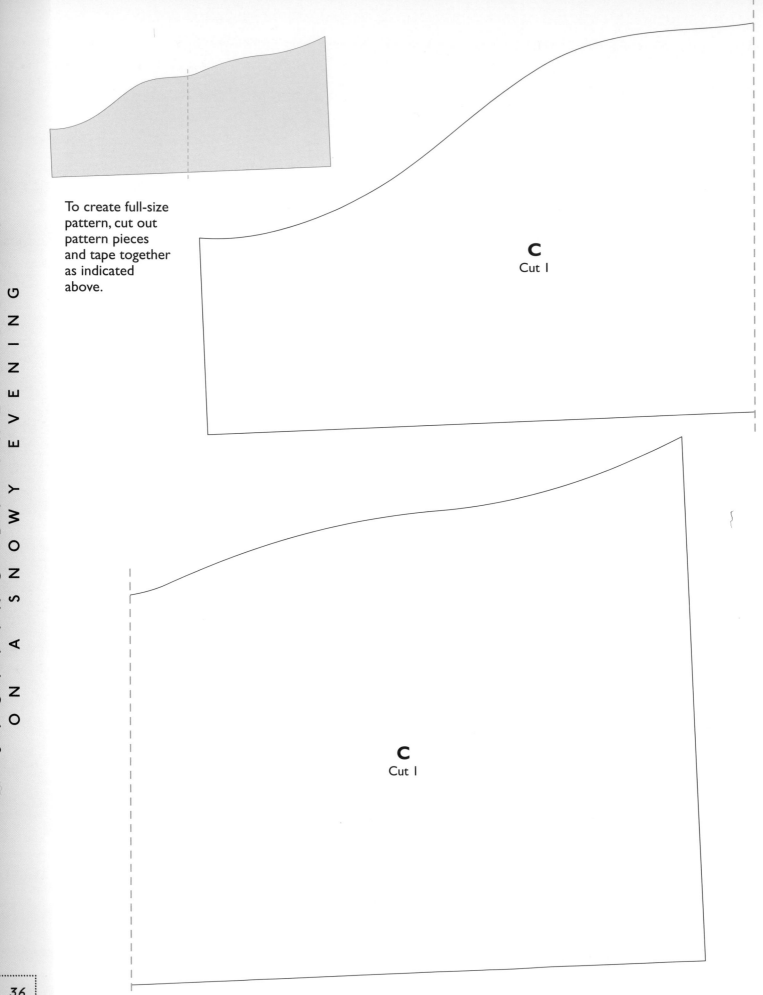

To create full-size
pattern, cut out
pattern pieces
and tape together
as indicated
above.

C
Cut 1

C
Cut 1

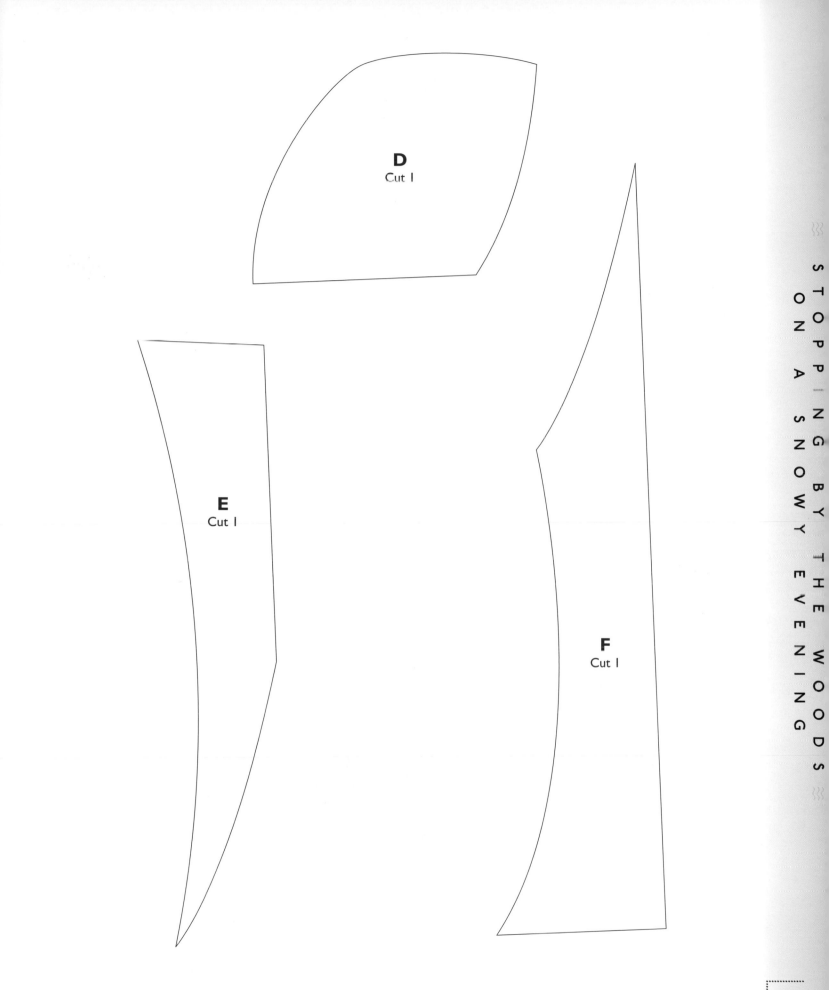

D
Cut 1

E
Cut 1

F
Cut 1

SNOW-FLAKES

Henry Wadworth Longfellow

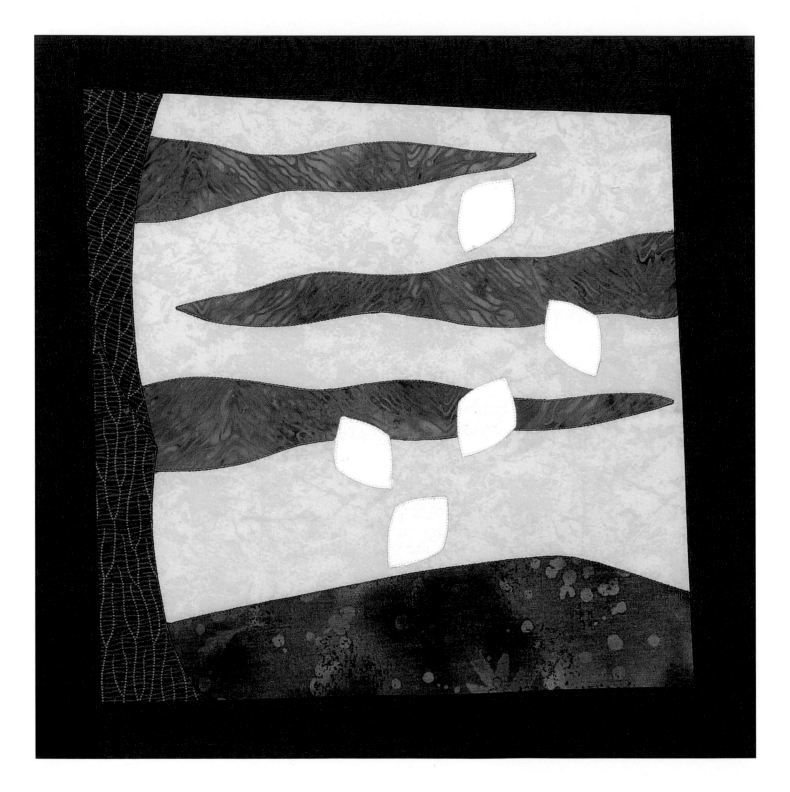

Out of the bosom of the Air,

Out of the cloud-folds of her garments shaken,

Over the woodlands brown and bare,

Over the harvest-fields forsaken,

Silent, and soft, and slow

Descends the snow.

Even as our cloudy fancies take

Suddenly shape in some divine expression,

Even as the troubled heart doth make

In the white countenance confession,

The troubled sky reveals

The grief it feels.

This is the poem of the air,

Slowly in silent syllables recorded;

This is the secret of despair,

Long in its cloudy bosom hoarded,

Now whispered and revealed

To wood and field.

Henry Wadsworth Longfellow
1807-1882

Though much of Longfellow's verse now sounds antiquated and quaint, he was, in fact, America's first "world-class" poet. Longfellow, whose ancestors came to this country on the Mayflower, created a uniquely American mythology with his poetry that remains a part of our collective national identity.

SNOW-FLAKES

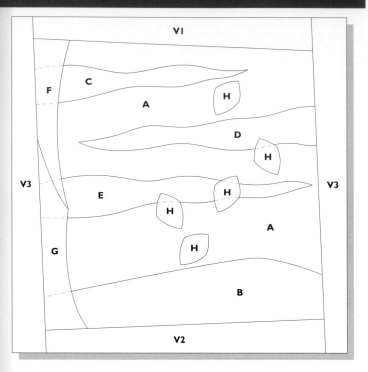

Finished block size: 14″ x 14″

Techniques: appliqué

Fabrics

Fat quarters (18″ x 22″)

- background A
- foreground B
- border

Scraps

- C, D, E clouds
- H snowflakes
- F, G tree

Directions

- Cut out background A and borders. Make freezer paper templates for B, C, D, E, F, G, and H (5)—fuse onto fabric. Cut pieces out and glue under edges that will show.
- Appliqué B to A.
- Appliqué C, D, E.
- Appliqué F, G.
- Add borders. Stitch borders on in this order: V1, V2, then V3s.
- Appliqué H snowflakes.

Tips:

The cloud shapes in this block offer endless design possibilities.

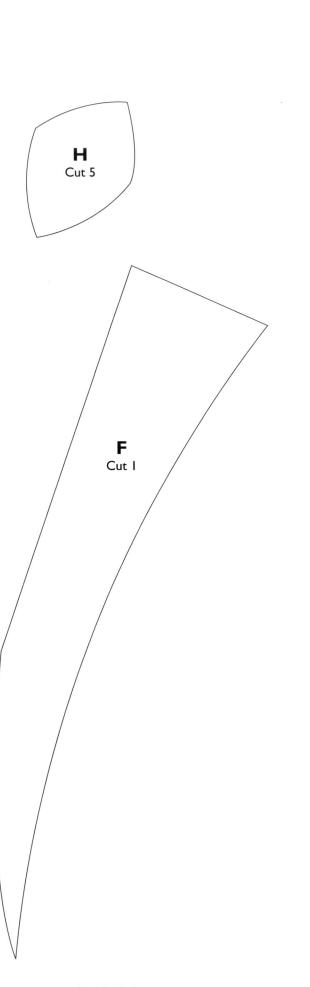

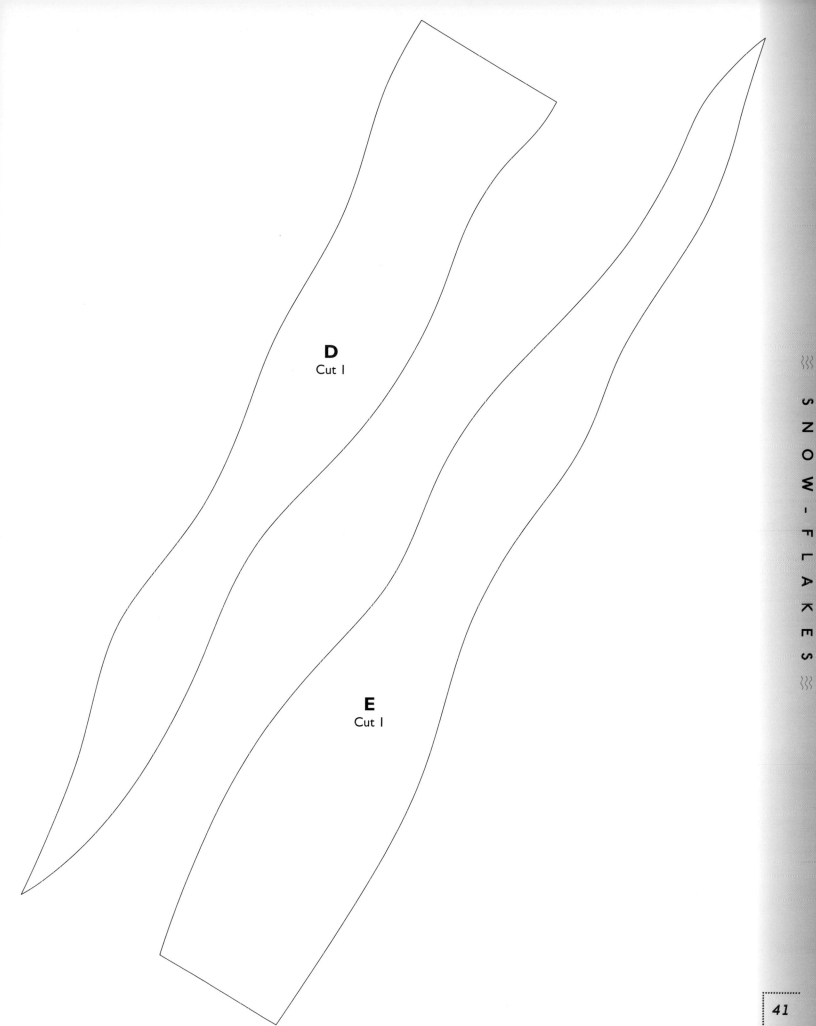

D
Cut 1

E
Cut 1

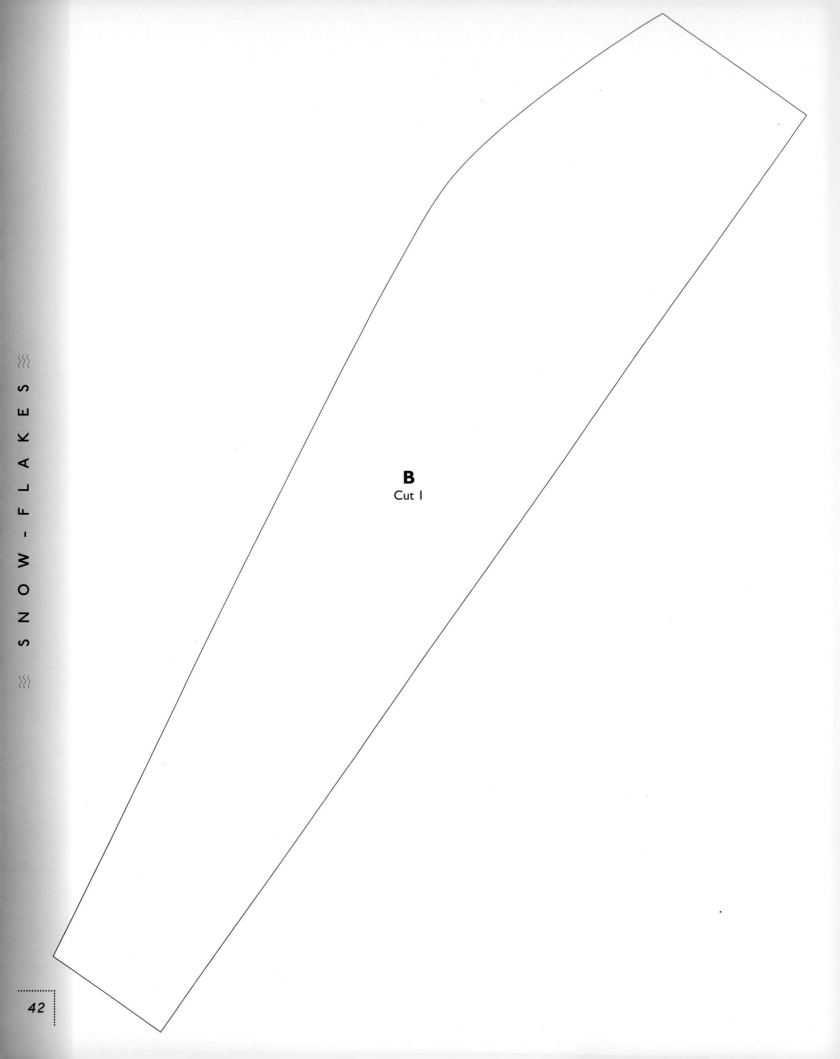

B
Cut I

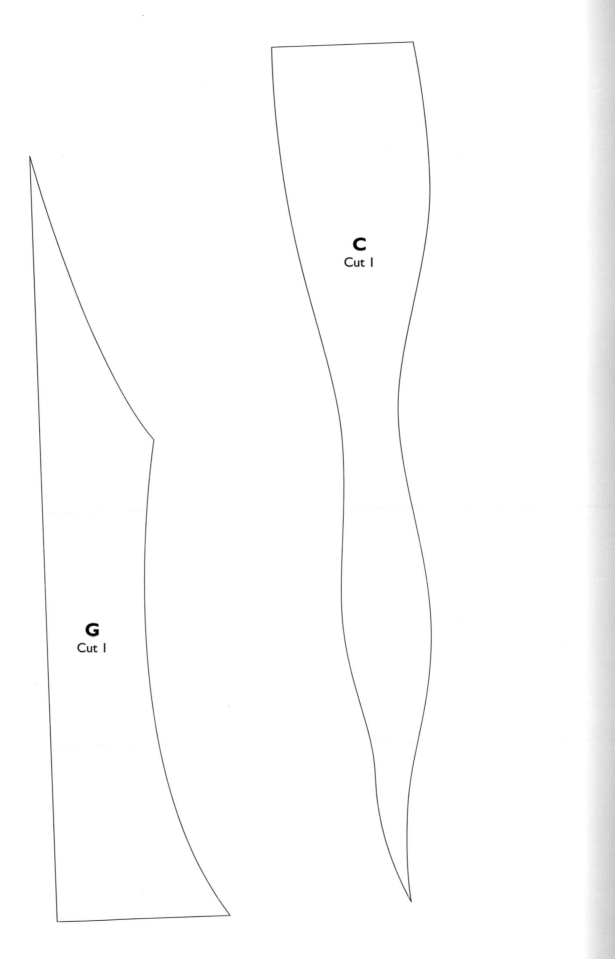

C
Cut 1

G
Cut 1

DREAMS

Langston Hughes

Hold fast to dreams
For if dreams die
Life is a broken-winged bird
That cannot fly.

Hold fast to dreams
For when dreams go
Life is a barren field
Frozen with snow.

Langston Hughes
1902–1967

*Langston Hughes was one of the
most prolific and influential
black writers
of the Twentieth century. He was
a successful novelist, playwright,
essayist and poet. His work
provided all Americans with deep
insights into the black
experience.
Hughes spent
much of his
boyhood in
Lawrence,
Kansas.*

DREAMS

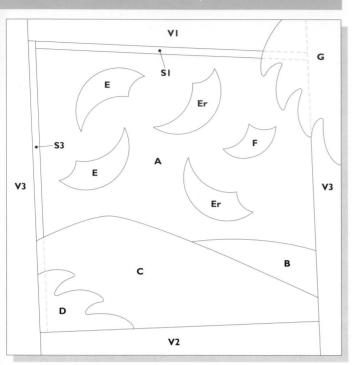

Size: 14″ x 14″

Techniques used: appliqué

Fabrics

Fat quarters (18″ x 22″)

- background
- border
- accent strips

Scraps:

- G, D wings
- 5 bright colors for E (2), Er (2), F

Directions

- Cut out background A and borders. Make freezer paper templates for B, C, D, E, F, G—fuse onto fabric. Cut pieces out and glue under edges that will show.
- Add S pieces. Pattern pieces is provided if you would like to piece or appliqué S. You can also try this: cut strip 1″ wide, 12 1/2″ long. Fold in half lengthwise, right sides out. Press. Cut strips 1″ wide.
  Cut S1 10 1/2″ long. Cut S3 9 1/4″ long. Fold in half lengthwise, right sides out. Press. Follow pattern and position in place on right side of background, edges together. Glue in place.
- Appliqué pieces to background A in this order: B, C, D.
- Add borders in this order: V1, V2, then V3s.
- Appliqué remaining pieces: E (2), Er (2), F and G.

Tips:

This block is designed to work with the next two blocks: *I Know Why the Caged Bird Sings* and *Dream Variations.* See pages 47 through 57.

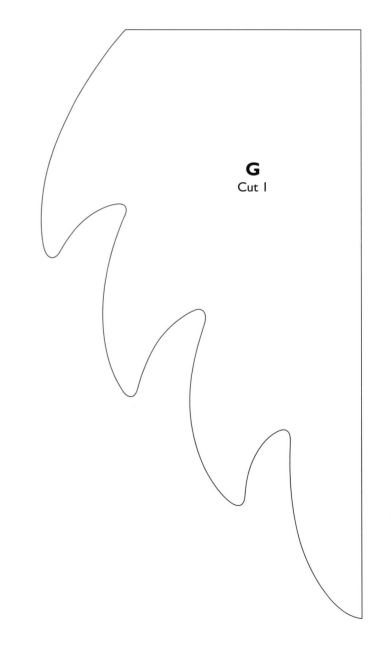

G
Cut 1

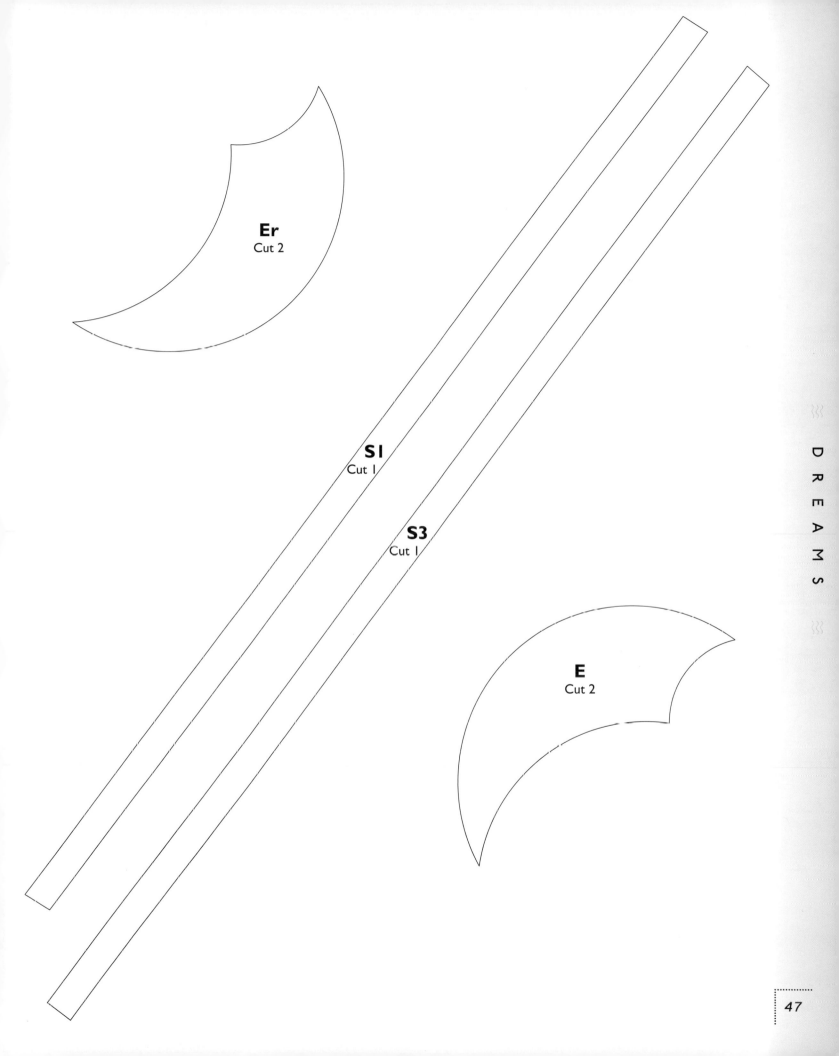

Er
Cut 2

S1
Cut 1

S3
Cut 1

E
Cut 2

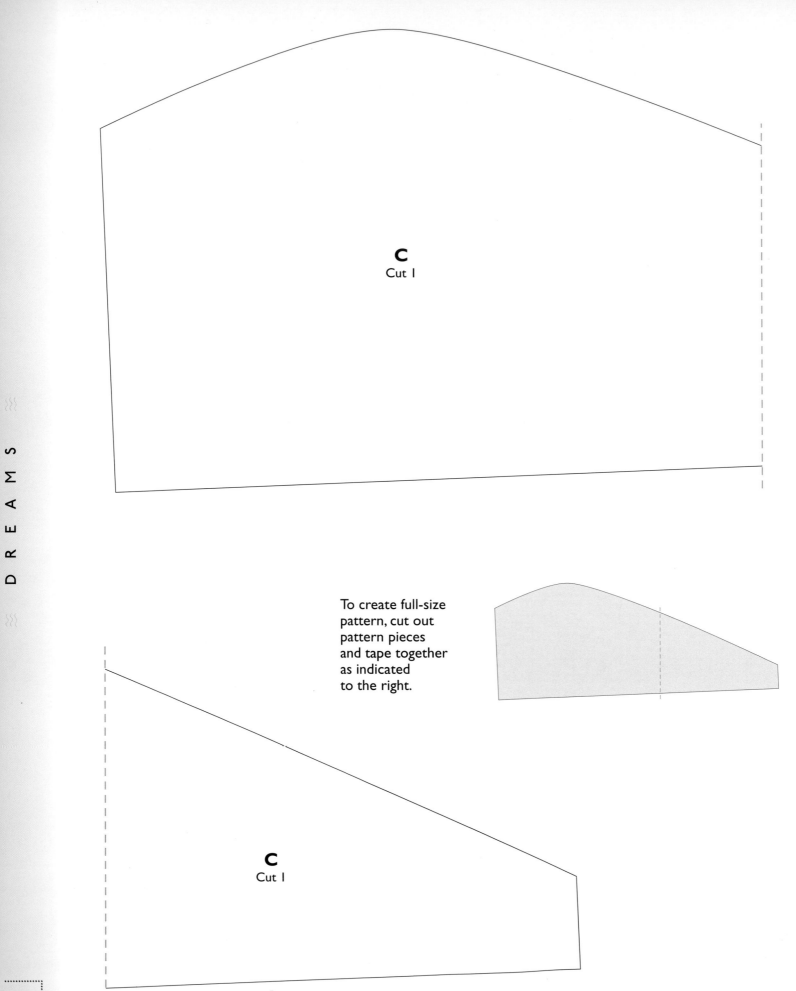

C
Cut 1

To create full-size
pattern, cut out
pattern pieces
and tape together
as indicated
to the right.

C
Cut 1

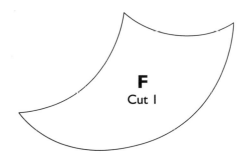

F
Cut 1

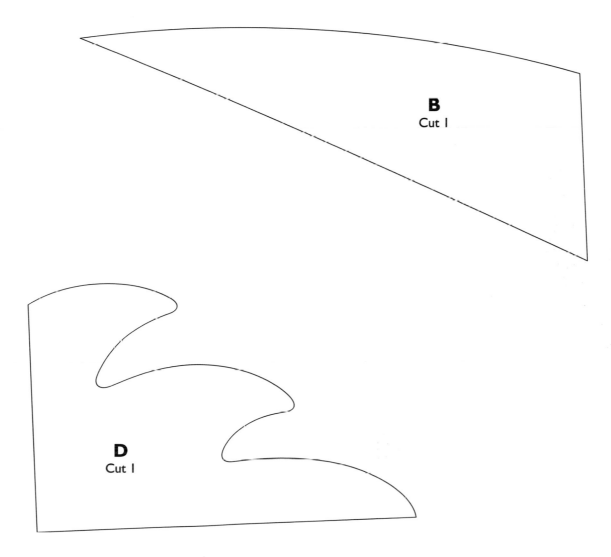

B
Cut 1

D
Cut 1

A free bird leaps on the back of the wind

and floats downstream till the current ends

and dips his wing in the orange suns rays and dares to claim

the sky.

But a bird that stalks down his narrow cage

can seldom see through his bars of rage

his wings are clipped and his feet are tied so he opens his

throat to sing.

The caged bird sings with a fearful trill

of things unknown but longed for still

and his tune is heard on the distant hill

for the caged bird sings of freedom.

The free bird thinks of another breeze

and the trade winds soft through the sighing trees

and the fat worms waiting on a dawn-bright lawn and he

names the sky his own.

But a caged bird stands on the grave of dreams

his shadow shouts on a nightmare scream

his wings are clipped and his feet are tied so he opens his

throat to sing.

The caged bird sings with a fearful trill

of things unknown but longed for still

and his tune is heard on the distant hill

for the caged bird sings of freedom.

Maya Angelou
1928–

Born Marguerite Johnson, Maya Angelou is a native of St. Louis. In addition to being one of America's most prolific and popular poets, Angelou has enjoyed a long career as an international journalist, a civil rights activist, a film and theater actor, and an educator. She served on the Bicentennial Commission under President Ford.

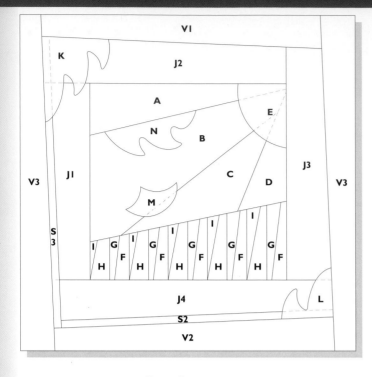

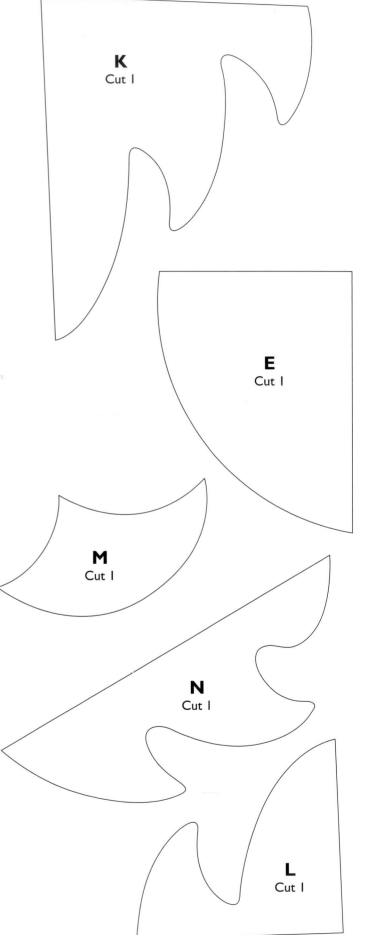

K Cut 1

E Cut 1

M Cut 1

N Cut 1

L Cut 1

Finished block size: 14″ x 14″

Techniques used: piecing, paper piecing, appliqué.

Fabrics

Fat quarters (18″ x 22″)

- inner borders
- outer borders
- accent strips

Scraps

- E sun
- K, L wings
- M, N birds
- A, B, C, D sky
- F, G, H, I cage

Directions

- Start with the center block. Paper piece A, B, C and D. Appliqué E, M and N as shown.
- Paper piece together bars (F,G,H,I). Trim to pattern size (plus 1/4″) when complete.
- Cut J border pieces. Stitch to sides. Press.
- Add accent strips. A pattern piece is provided if you want to piece or appliqué S2 and S3. You can also try this: cut strip 1″ wide, 12 1/2″ long. Fold in half lengthwise, right sides out. Press. Cut strips 1″ wide. Cut S2 10 1/2″ long. Cut S3 10″ long. Fold in half lengthwise, right sides out. Press. Follow pattern and position in place on right side of background, edges together. Glue in place.
- Appliqué K and L to corners.
- Add borders in this order: V1, V2, then V3s.

Tips:

Random strip piecing would work for bars piece (F, G, H and I). This block was designed to work with *Dreams* (see page 40) and *Dream Variations* (see page 52).

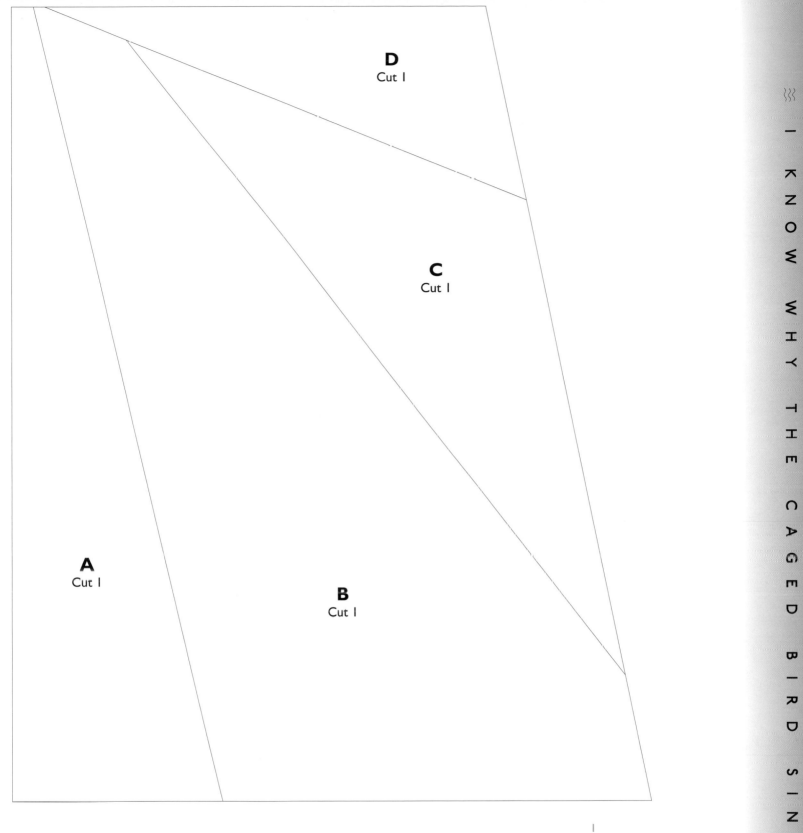

D
Cut 1

C
Cut 1

A
Cut 1

B
Cut 1

S2 Cut 1

S2 Cut 1

S3 Cut 1

S3 Cut 1

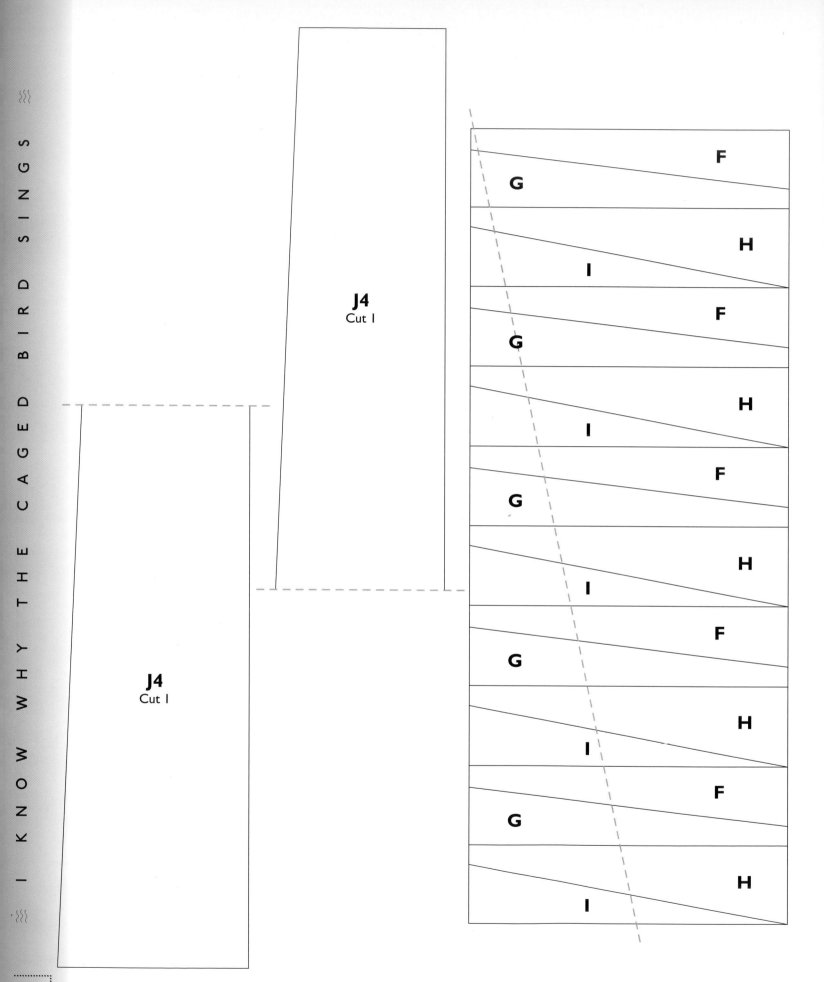

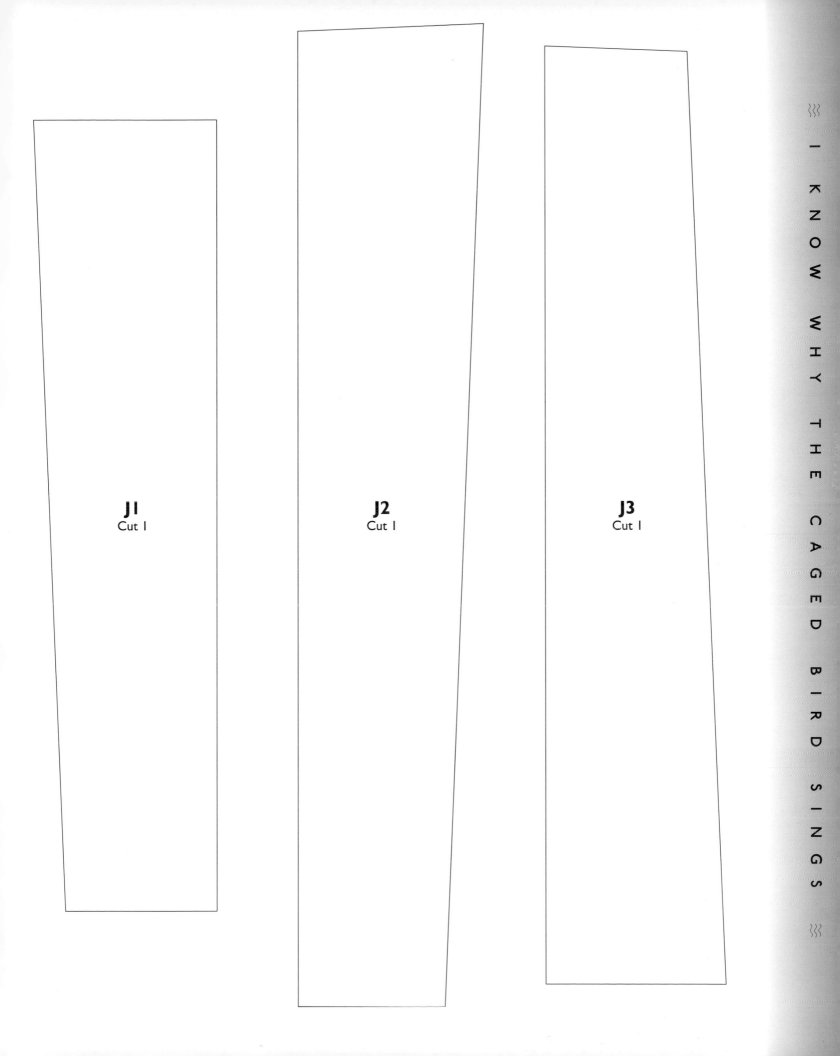

J1
Cut 1

J2
Cut 1

J3
Cut 1

To fling my arms wide

In some place of the sun,

To whirl and to dance

Till the white day is done.

Then rest at cool evening

Beneath a tall tree

While night comes on gently,

    Dark like me—

That is my dream!

To fling my arms wide

In the face of the sun,

Dance! Whirl! Whirl!

Till the quick day is done.

Rest at pale evening . . .

A tall, slim tree . . .

Night coming tenderly

    Black like me.

Langston Hughes
1902-1967

Because he was worried that his son wouldn't be able to support himself as a writer, Langston Hughes' father agreed to pay his college tuition only if he majored in engineering.

Hughes was an aficionado of jazz and blues. His poems were often written in jazz rhythms. In a short auto-biographical sketch Hughes once wrote, "I like... goat's milk, short novels, lyric poems, heat, simple folk, boats and bullfights; I dislike... parsnips, long novels, narrative poems, cold, pretentious folk, buses and bridges."

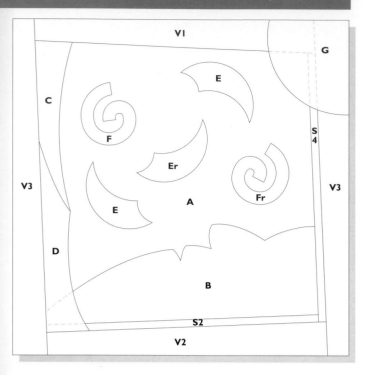

Finished block size: 14″ x 14″

Technique used: appliqué

Fabrics

Fat quarters (18″ x 22″)

- border
- background A
- B face

Scraps:

- G sun
- C, D tree trunk
- 5 brights for sky — E, Er, F, Fr

Directions

- Cut out background A and borders. Make freezer paper templates for B, C, D, E (2), Er, F, Fr, G—fuse onto fabric.

  Cut pieces out and glue under edges that will show.

- Appliqué B to background A.

- Add S pieces. A pattern piece is provided if you would like to piece or appliqué S. You can also try this: cut strip 1″ wide, 12 1/2″ long. Fold in half lengthwise, right sides out. Press. Cut strips 1″ wide. Cut S2 11″ long, cut S4 10″ long. Fold in half lengthwise, right sides out. Press. Follow pattern and position in place on right side of background, edges together. Glue in place.

- Appliqué C and D.

- Add borders in this order: V1, V2, then V3s.

- Appliqué E (2), Er, F, Fr, and G as shown.

Tips:

This block is designed to work with *Dreams* (see page 40) and *I Know Why the Caged Bird Sings* (see page 46).

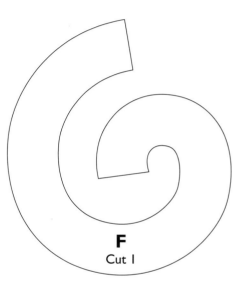

F
Cut 1

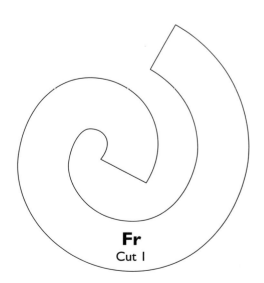

Fr
Cut 1

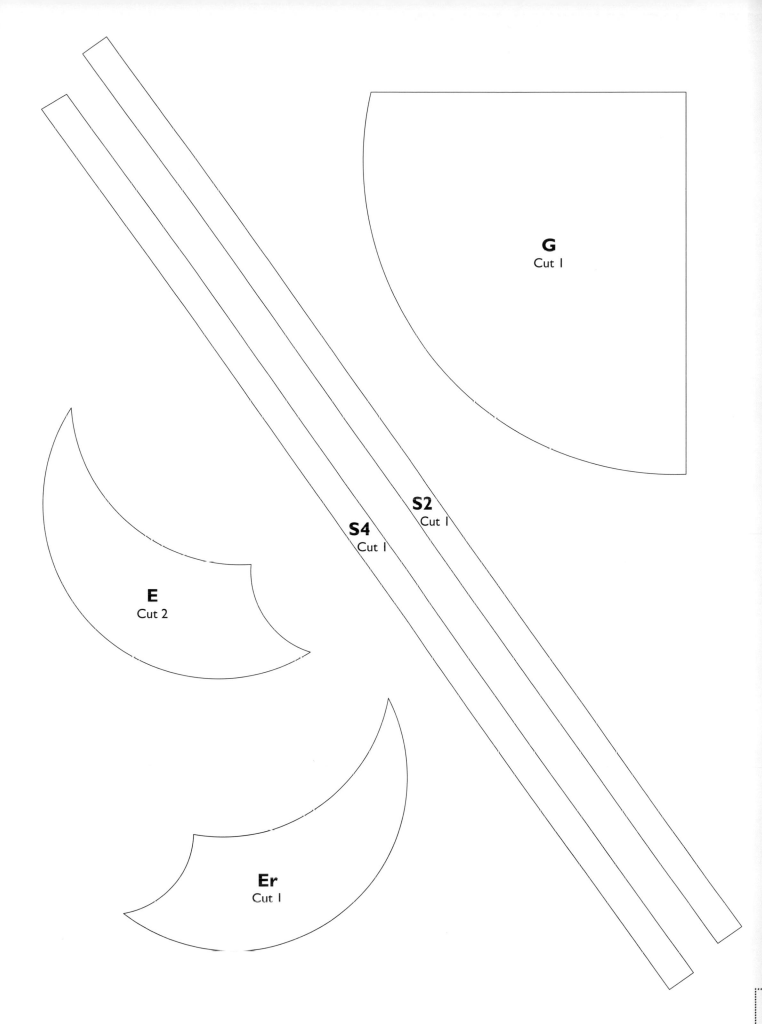

G
Cut 1

S2
Cut 1

S4
Cut 1

E
Cut 2

Er
Cut 1

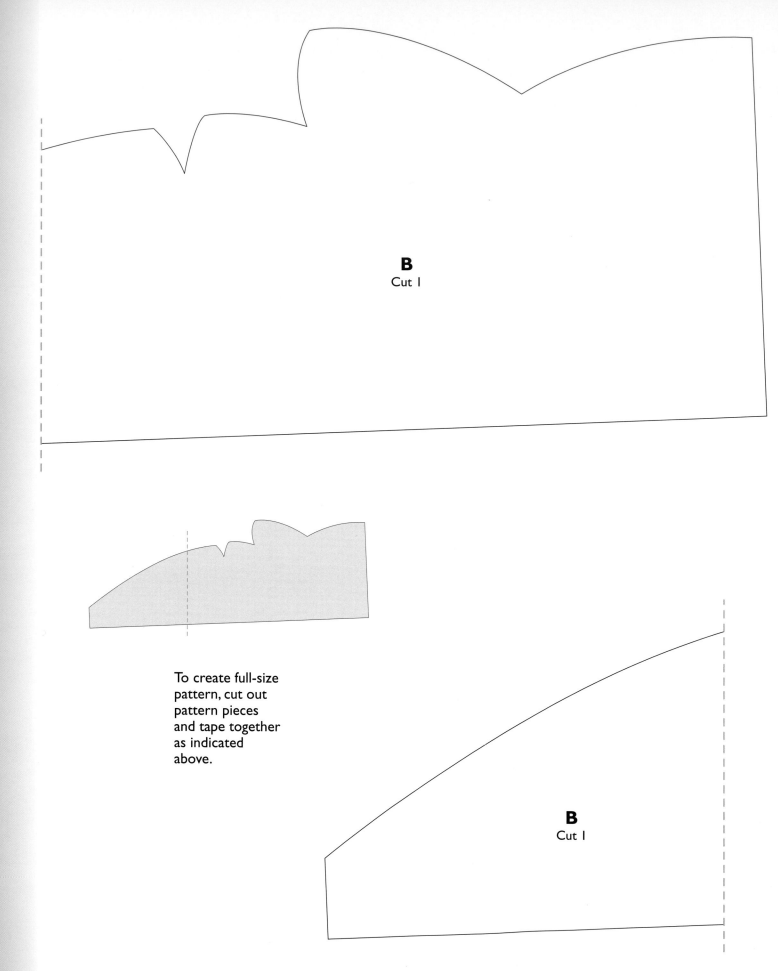

B
Cut 1

To create full-size
pattern, cut out
pattern pieces
and tape together
as indicated
above.

B
Cut 1

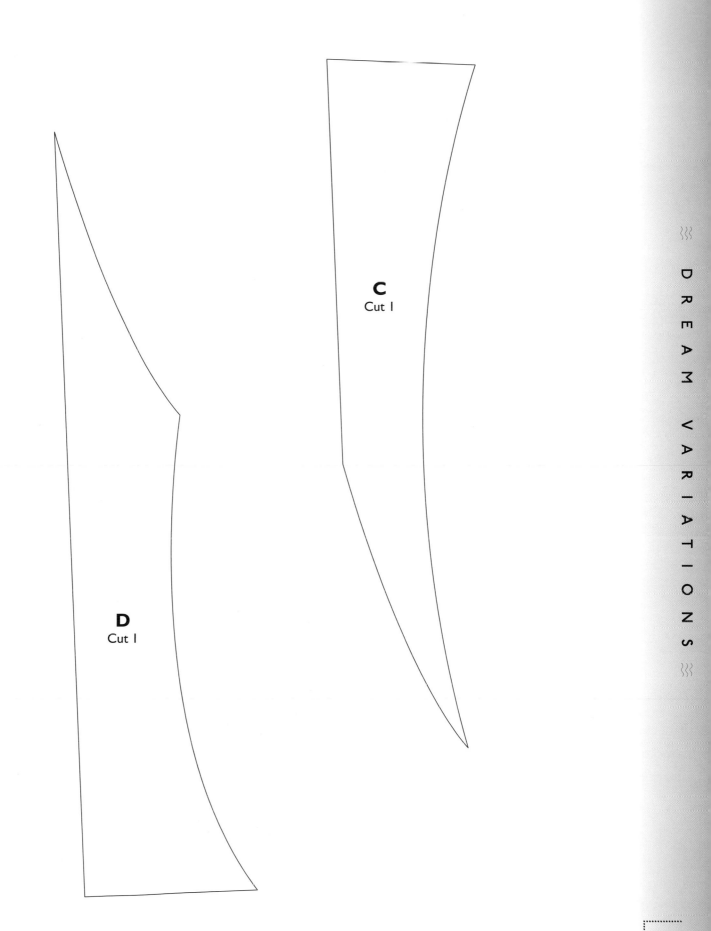

C
Cut 1

D
Cut 1

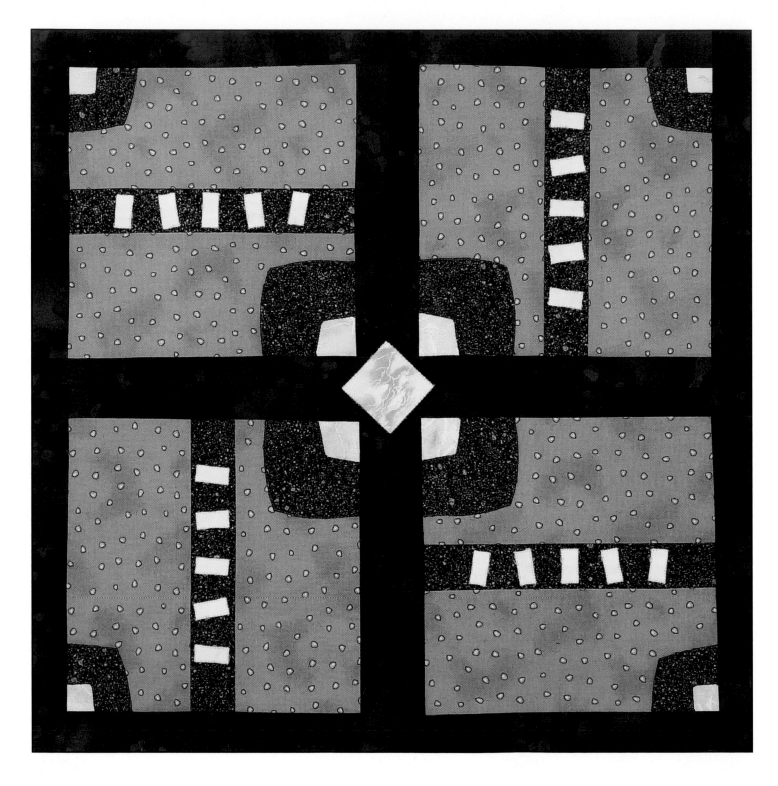

The fog comes
on little cat feet.

It sits looking
over harbor and city
on silent haunches
and then moves on.

Carl Sandburg
1878-1967

Carl Sandburg was a giant of American letters. An advertising copywriter, journalist, scholar, folksinger and poet, he celebrated the life of the great Abraham Lincoln in a six-volume biography and the lives of common American laborers and farmers in his gritty and witty poetry.

FOG

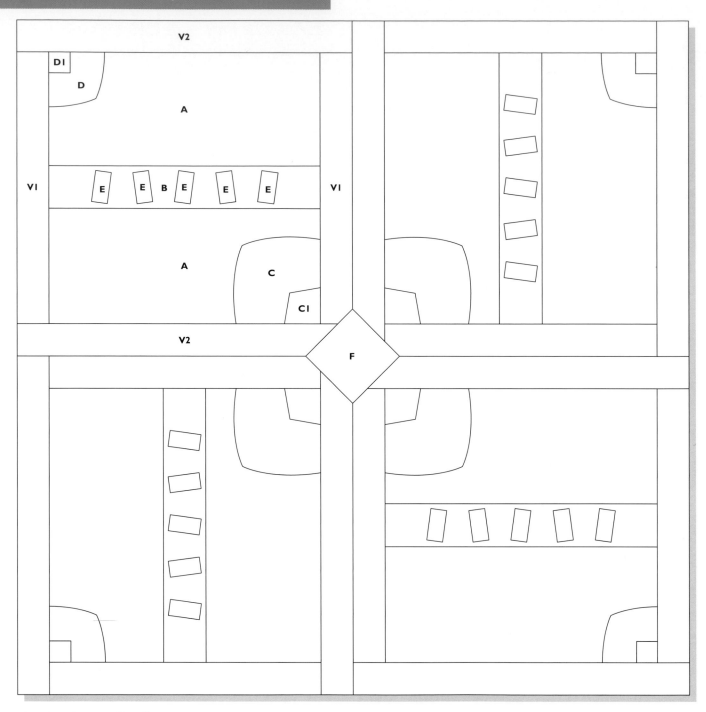

Finished block size: 7″ x 7″

Techniques: piecing, appliqué

Fabrics

Fat quarters (18″ x 22″)

- background A
- center strip B
- border

Scraps

- C, C1, D, D1 shapes
- E rectangles

Directions

- Piece A (2) and B.
- Place accent C1, D1 in corners. Glue/pin in place.
- Appliqué C and D.
- Appliqué five E rectangles.
- Add borders V1 (2) then V2 (2).
- Stitch four blocks—arrange as shown. Final size of four blocks is 14″ x 14″.
- Appliqué F at intersection of blocks.

Tips:

Lots of variation is possible for arranging this basic block.

Appliqué F at intersections where corners meet.

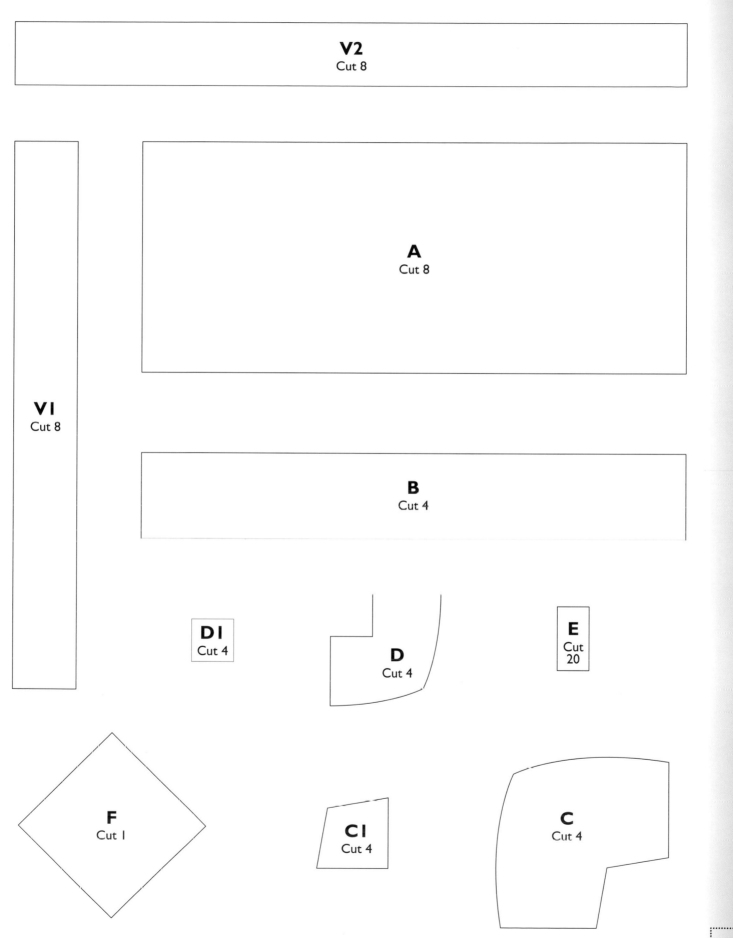

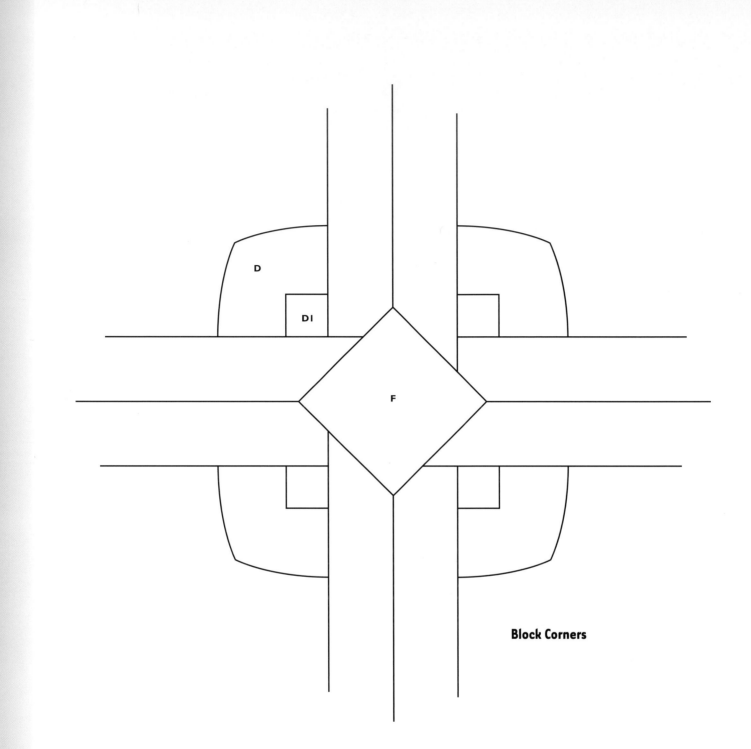

Block Corners

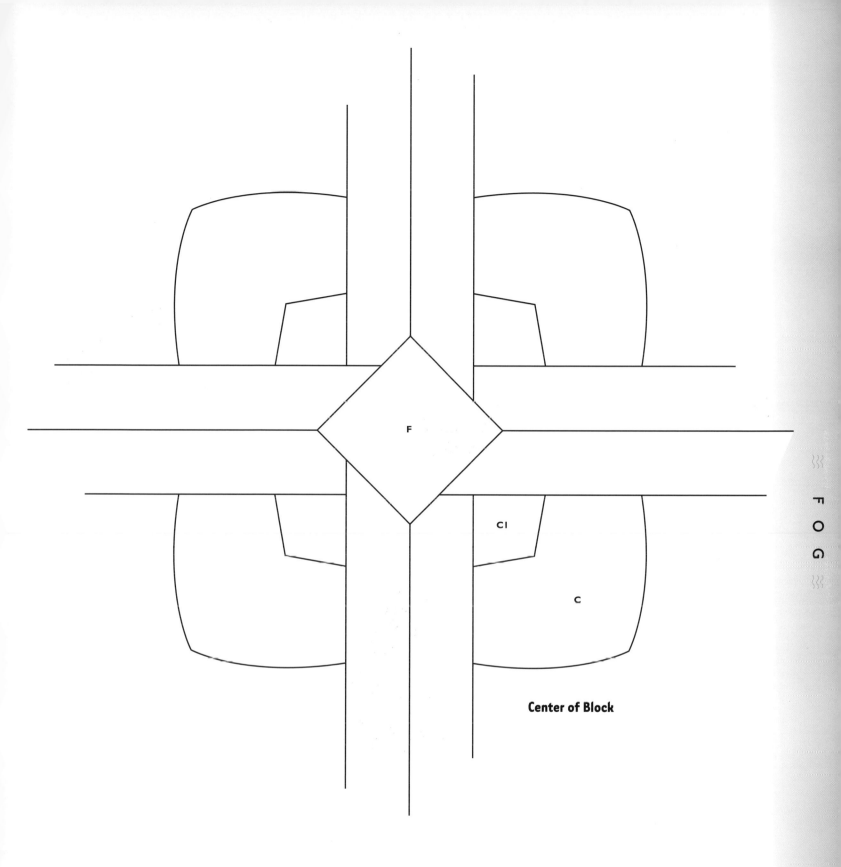

Center of Block

A gentle boy, with soft and silken locks

A dreamy boy, with brown and tender eyes,

A castle-builder, with his wooden blocks,

And towers that touch imaginary skies.

A fearless rider on his father's knee,

An eager listener unto stories told

At the Round Table of the nursery,

Of heroes and adventures manifold.

There will be other towers for thee to build;

There will be other steeds for thee to ride;

There will be other legends, and all filled

With greater marvels and more glorified.

Build on, and make thy castles high and fair,

Rising and reaching upward to the skies;

Listen to voices in the upper air,

Nor lose thy simple faith in mysteries.

Henry Wadsworth Longfellow
1807-1882

Longfellow was among the first American poets to actually write about America. He wrote about our history and traditions, our geography, and our people. Until Longfellow and his generation of fellow writers, most of the literature, art, and music enjoyed by Americans came from Europe. When the city of Cambridge, Massachusetts determined it was necessary to remove "the spreading chestnut tree" to which Longfellow referred in his poem "The Village Blacksmith," the children of the town collected pennies to have a chair built from the tree as a gift to Longfellow.

THE CASTLE-BUILDER

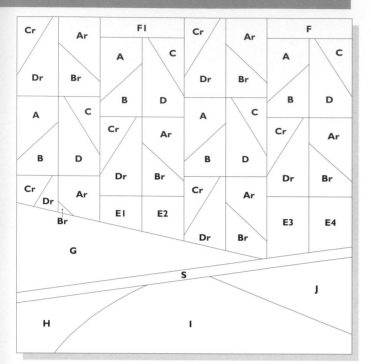

Finished block size: 14″ x 14″

Techniques: piecing

Fabrics

Fat quarters (18″ x 22″)

- foreground G, I
- accent S

Scraps:

- foreground H, J
- castles B, D, Dr, Br, F, F1
- sky A, C, Cr, Ar

Directions

- Piece: 4 A/B blocks, 4 C/D blocks, 5 Ar/Br blocks, 1 partial Ar, Br block, 5 Cr/Dr blocks, 1 partial Cr, Dr block. Assemble in vertical strips as shown: stitch.
- Stitch E and F blocks to ends of pieced units.
- Attach G.
- Attach S.
- Piece H and I to J. Stitch to S.

Tips:

This is paper-pieced in vertical rows. We stitched each row, then stitched two rows together and added F pieces, then joined those units. We used freezer paper templates for the foreground, which helped those pieces fit together accurately.

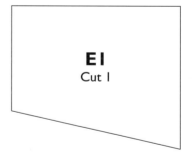

E1
Cut 1

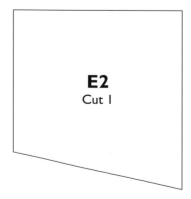

E2
Cut 1

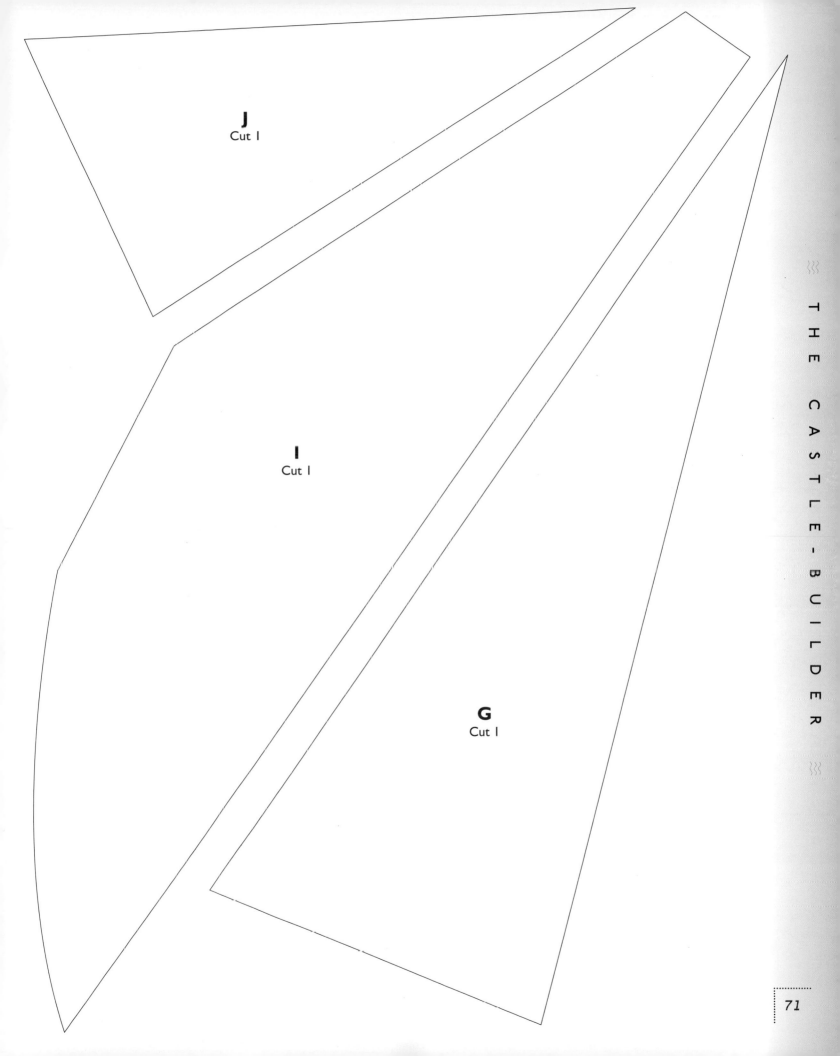

J
Cut 1

I
Cut 1

G
Cut 1

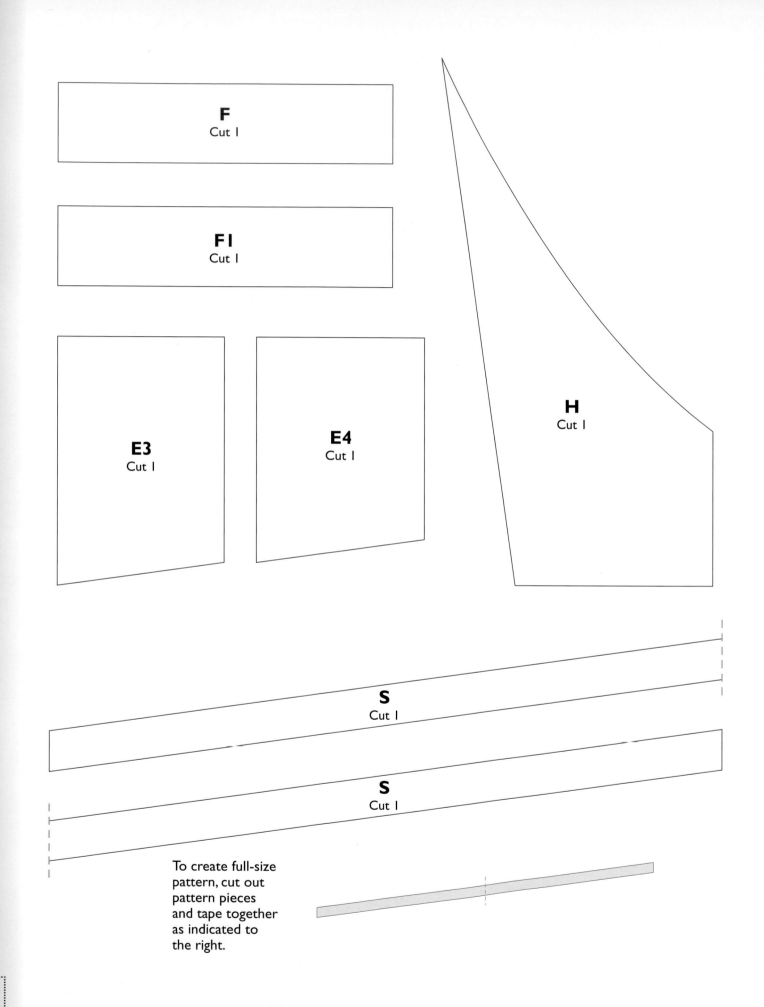

F
Cut 1

F1
Cut 1

E3
Cut 1

E4
Cut 1

H
Cut 1

S
Cut 1

S
Cut 1

To create full-size pattern, cut out pattern pieces and tape together as indicated to the right.

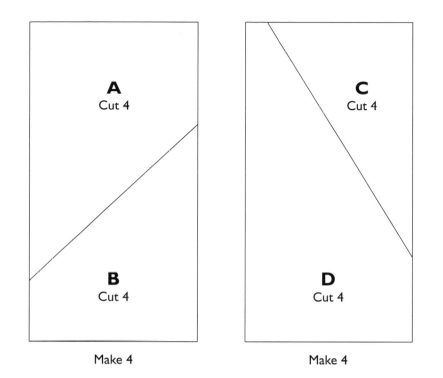

A
Cut 4

B
Cut 4

Make 4

C
Cut 4

D
Cut 4

Make 4

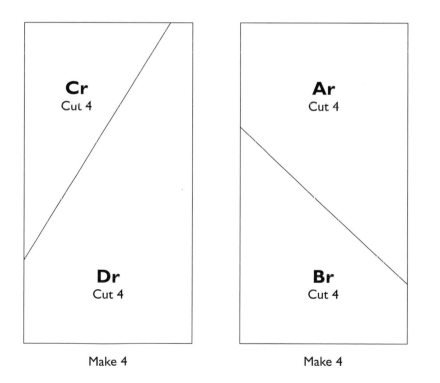

Cr
Cut 4

Dr
Cut 4

Make 4

Ar
Cut 4

Br
Cut 4

Make 4

Safe upon the solid rock the ugly houses stand:

Come and see my shining palace built upon the sand!

Edna St. Vincent Millay
1892-1950

Millay, who was called "Vincent" by her family and friends, was a graduate of Vassar College. She was the first woman to win the Pulitzer Prize (1923). During one particularly creative period she lived in a nine-foot long attic in Greenwich Village in New York City.

SECOND FIG

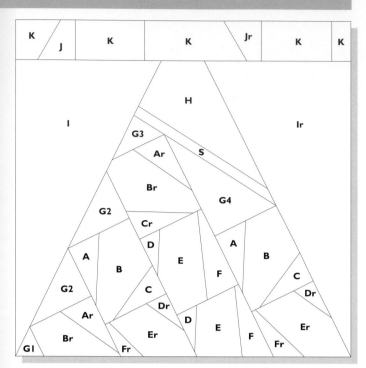

Finished block size: 14″ x 14″

Techniques: piecing, appliqué

Fabrics

Fat quarters (18″ x 22″)

• background I, Ir

Scraps:

• brights for center pieced area

• subdued colors for top pieced strip

Directions

• Start with center triangle. There are four blocks used: A/B/C, D/E/F, and the reverse of those blocks. Piece: 2 A/B/C blocks and 2 D/E/F blocks, 2 Ar/Br/Cr blocks and 2 Dr/Er/Fr blocks. G pieces are provided or cut 3 1/2″ to piece at ends of strips. Paper piece each block individually, then assemble in strips as shown: stitch all together. Press at every step. Stitch S on, then H. Add I, Ir pieces. Trim block edges to square it off.

• Pattern pieces are provided for the top pieced row—or use 2 1/4″ strips, with the J/Jr triangles added. Piece as shown, press. Stitch to rest of block.

Tips:

An alternative is to use this design as a starting point. Cut strips 3 1/2″ wide. Cut into blocks and piece irregular triangles on corners. Make your own design.

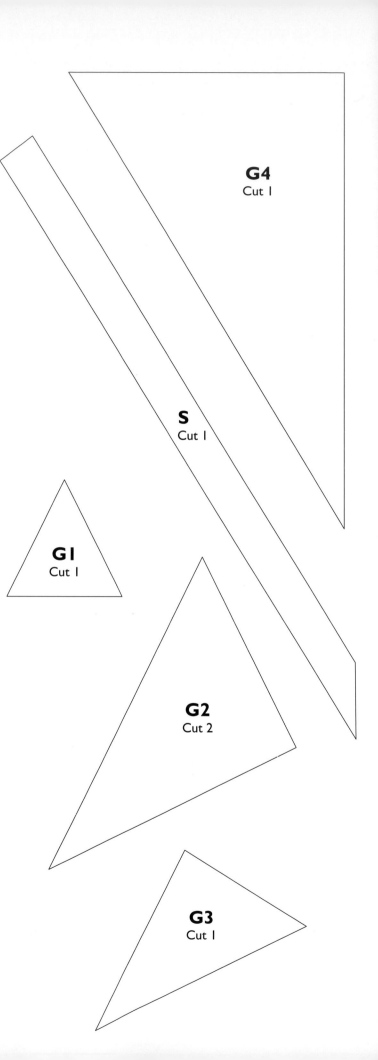

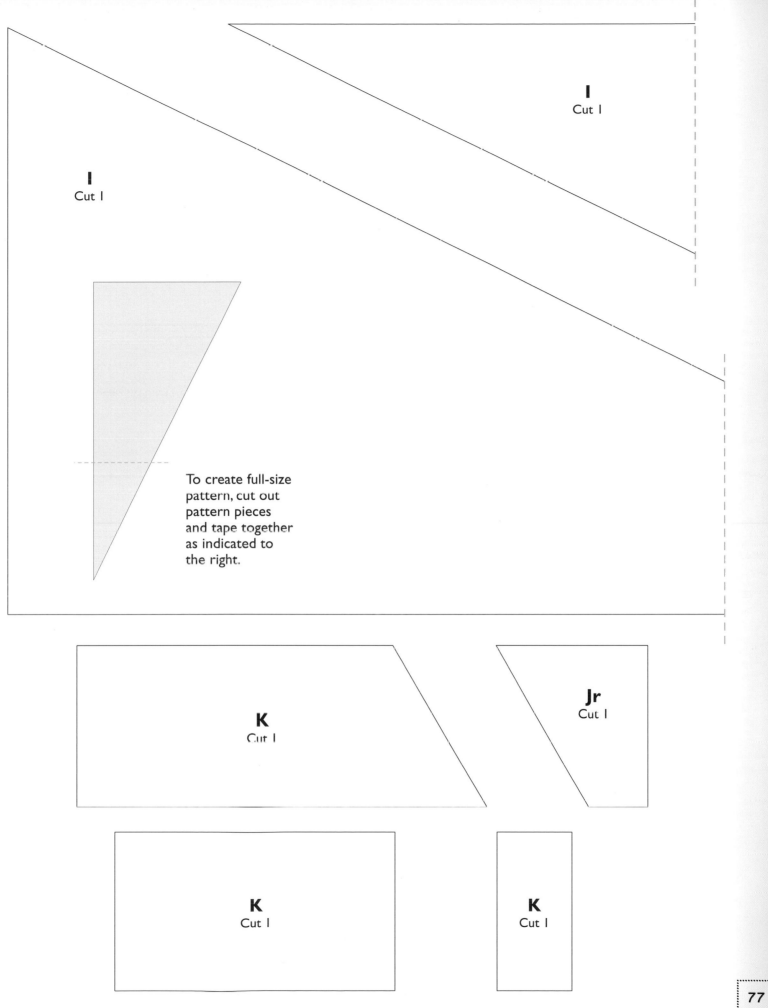

I
Cut 1

I
Cut 1

To create full-size
pattern, cut out
pattern pieces
and tape together
as indicated to
the right.

K
Cut 1

Jr
Cut 1

K
Cut 1

K
Cut 1

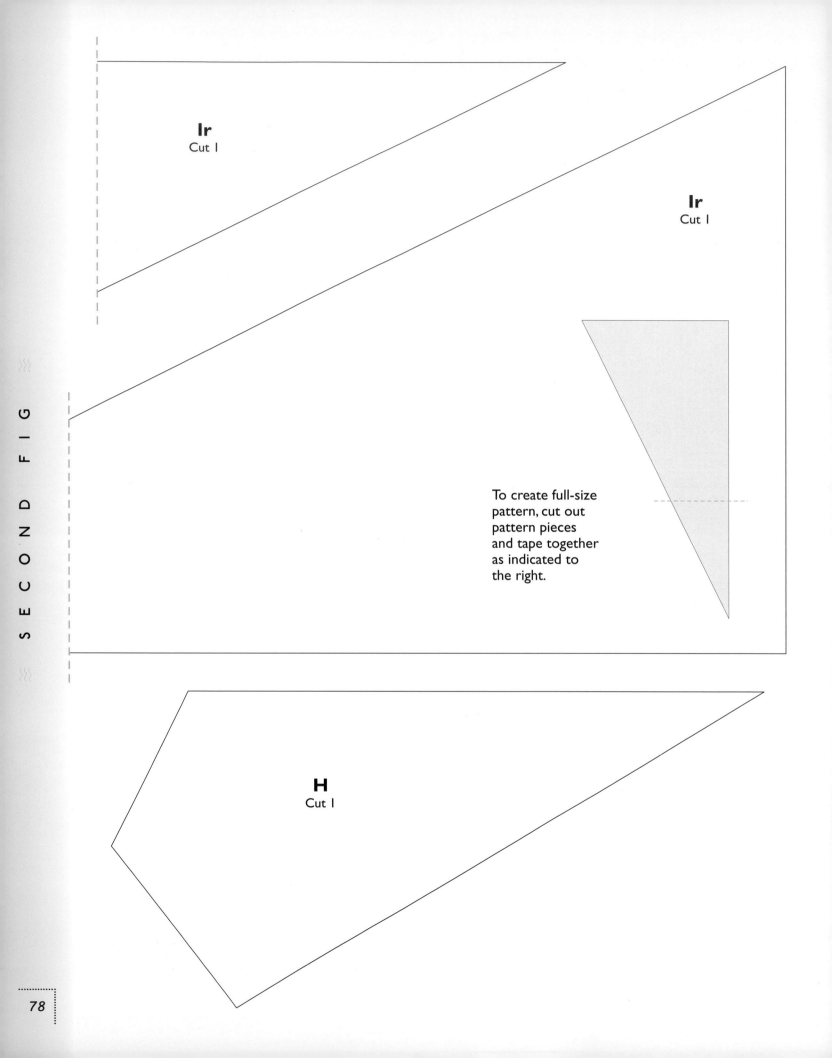

Ir
Cut 1

Ir
Cut 1

To create full-size pattern, cut out pattern pieces and tape together as indicated to the right.

H
Cut 1

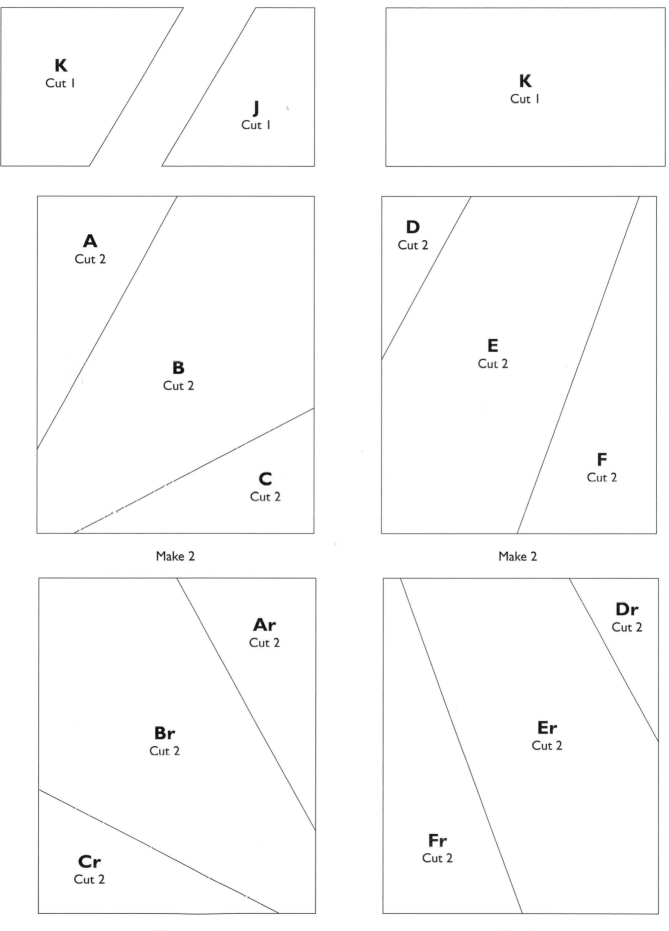

K
Cut 1

J
Cut 1

K
Cut 1

A
Cut 2

B
Cut 2

C
Cut 2

Make 2

D
Cut 2

E
Cut 2

F
Cut 2

Make 2

Ar
Cut 2

Br
Cut 2

Cr
Cut 2

Make 2

Dr
Cut 2

Er
Cut 2

Fr
Cut 2

Make 2

The way a crow

Shook down on me

The dust of snow

From a hemlock tree

Has given my heart

A change of mood

And saved some part

Of a day I had rued.

Robert Frost
1874-1963

*In addition to writing poetry,
Frost wrote occasional articles
for poultry journals. Frost recited
from memory his poem "The Gift
Outright" at the 1960
inauguration of President John F.
Kennedy. When Frost died in
October of 1963, Kennedy
honored Frost's poetry by saying,
"its tide... lifts all spirits." He
said of Frost, his
"sense of the
human tragedy
fortified him
against
self-deception
and easy
consolation."*

DUST OF SNOW

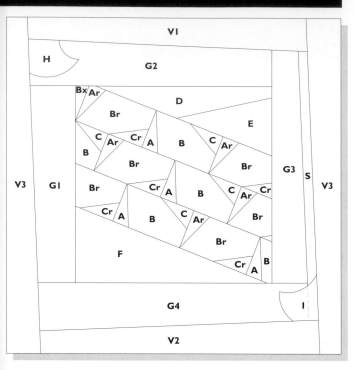

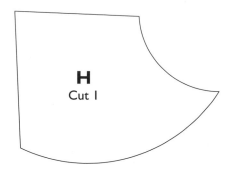

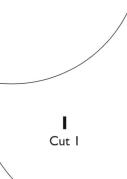

Finished block size: 14″ x 14″

Techniques used: piecing, appliqué

Fabrics

Fat quarters (18″ x 22″)
- inner border
- outer border

Scraps:
- for center block
- H, I hemlock
- accent strip

Directions

- Start with center block. Piece: 3 complete and 2 partial A/B/C blocks and 6 Ar/Br/Cr blocks. Add Bx where indicated. Assemble as shown: stitch. Piece D and E: stitch to one side of block. Stitch F to other side of block. Press at every step. Trim block edges to square it off.
- Add inner borders: G1, G2, G3 and G4.
- Add accent strip. A pattern piece is provided if you would like to piece or appliqué this piece on. You can also try this: cut a strip 1″ wide. Cut S 11″ long. Fold in half lengthwise, right sides out. Press. Position in place on right side of matching border piece G3, with cut edges together. Glue in place.
- Add borders in this order V1, V2, then V3s.
- Appliqué H and I as shown.

Tips:

The colors of winter on the prairie inspired this block. The border fabric seemed to capture them all and we worked from there.

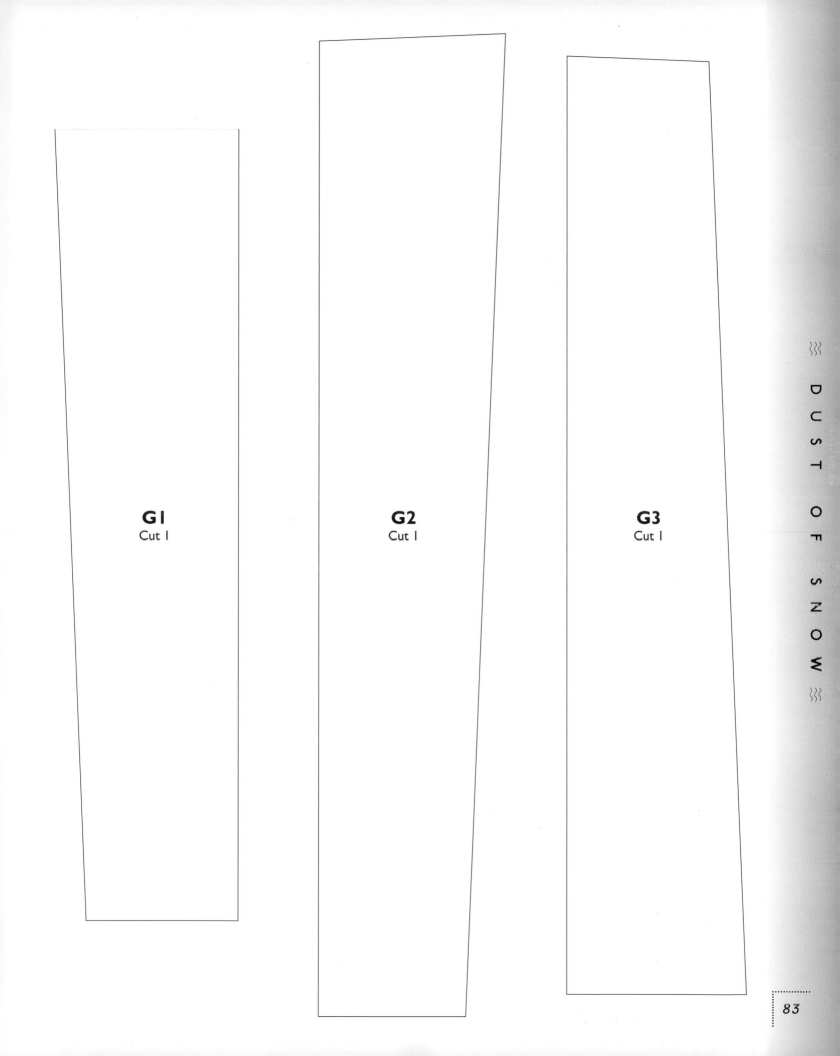

G1
Cut 1

G2
Cut 1

G3
Cut 1

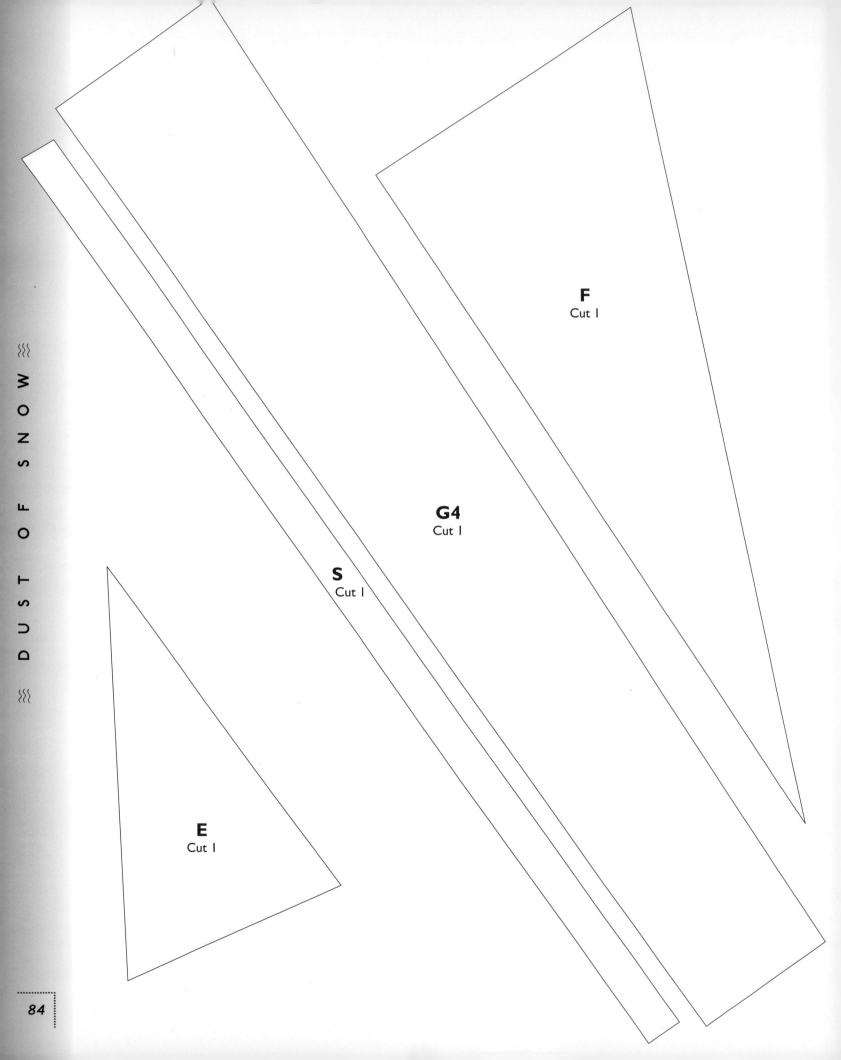

F
Cut 1

G4
Cut 1

S
Cut 1

E
Cut 1

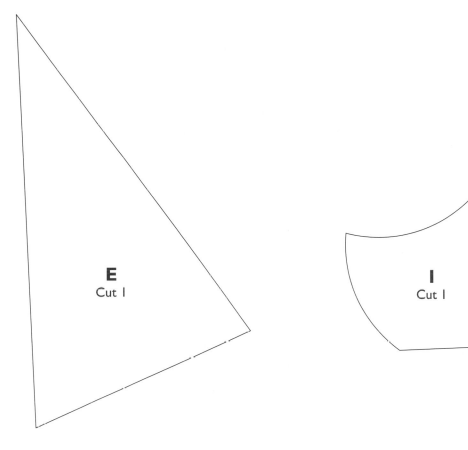

E
Cut 1

I
Cut 1

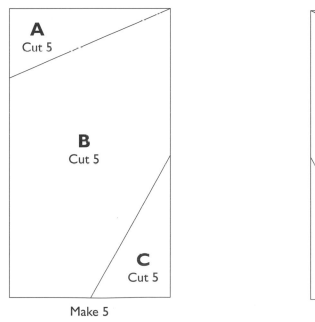

A
Cut 5

B
Cut 5

C
Cut 5

Make 5

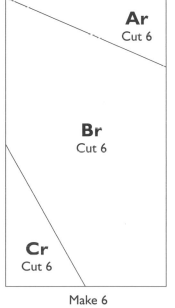

Ar
Cut 6

Br
Cut 6

Cr
Cut 6

Make 6

"Hope" is the thing with feathers

That perches in the soul

And sings the tune without the words

And never stops at all,

And sweetest in the gale is heard;

And sore must be the storm

That could abash the little bird

That kept so many warm.

I've heard it in the chillest land

And on the strangest sea,

Yet never, in extremity,

It asked a crumb of me.

Emily Dickinson
1830-1886

Emily Dickinson's poems were unpublished during her lifetime and therefore unknown except to her family and friends. The first of her works were published four years after her death. Her poems reflect the extraordinary isolation and loneliness of her life, though they also reveal a deep hopefulness and abiding faith.

FIRST FIG

Edna St. Vincent Millay

Finishe

Techniq

Fabrics

Fat q

- inn
- out

Scrap

- for
- fea
- acc
- acc

Directio

- Sta
  A/B
  Ass
  at e
- Add
- Add
  like
  cut
  side
  bor
- Add
- App

Tips:

We chos

coordin

colored

My candle burns at both ends;

It will not last the night;

But ah, my foes, and oh, my friends--

It gives a lovely light!

Edna St. Vincent Millay
1892-1950

After flirting with socialism and pacifism as a young adult, Millay became an ardent supporter of the Allied cause during World War II. Some biographies incorrectly state that Millay died falling down stairs at her home and breaking her neck. In fact, she died of heart failure.

FIRST FIG

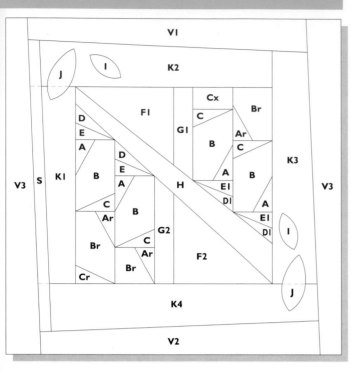

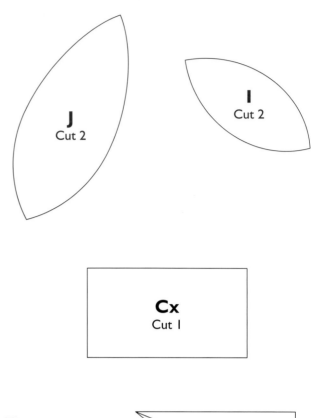

Finished block size: 14″ x 14″

Techniques used: piecing, appliqué

Fabrics

Fat quarters (18″ x 22″)

- inner border
- outer border

Scraps:

- we used black, gold, orange, blue, yellow, red
- center strip H
- accent strip S

Directions

- Start with center block. Piece: 4 A/B/C blocks, 1 complete Ar/Br/Cr blocks, 2 partial Ar/Br/Cr blocks, 2 D/E blocks, and 2 D1/E1 blocks. Add Cx where indicated. Assemble as shown: stitch. Add G and G1 strips, then F1 and F2. Press at every step.
- Join center pieced areas with H strip. Press. Trim block edges so it's square.
- Add inner borders: K1, K2, K3 and K4.
- Add accent strip. A pattern piece is provided if you would like to piece or appliqué S. You can also try this: cut strip 1″ wide, 12 1/2″ long. Fold in half lengthwise, right sides out. Press. Position in place on right side of matching border piece K1 (plus K2 and K4 ends) with cut edges together. Glue in place.
- Add borders in this order: V1, V2, then V3s.
- Appliqué I (2) and J(2) as shown.

Tips:

Note: some of these blocks are turned upside down: A/B/C is one. Also note: F1 and F2 and the D and E pieces are different sizes too. There are so many ways to color this block! We worked to make sure there was contrast between the different colors so the pieces would show.

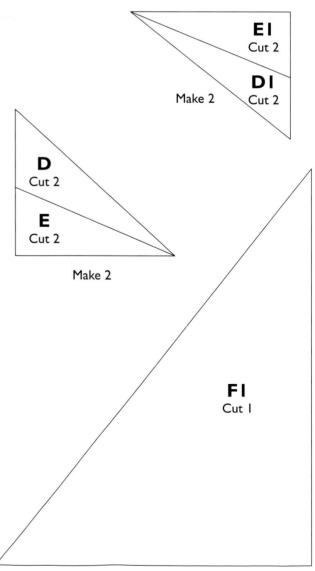

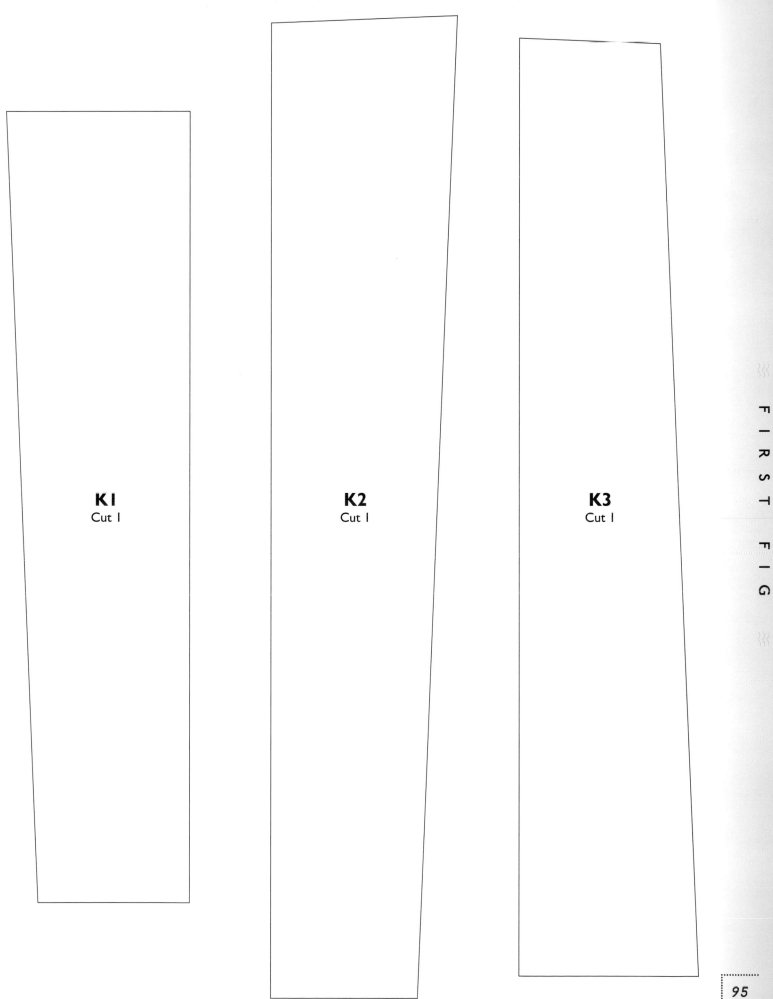

K1
Cut 1

K2
Cut 1

K3
Cut 1

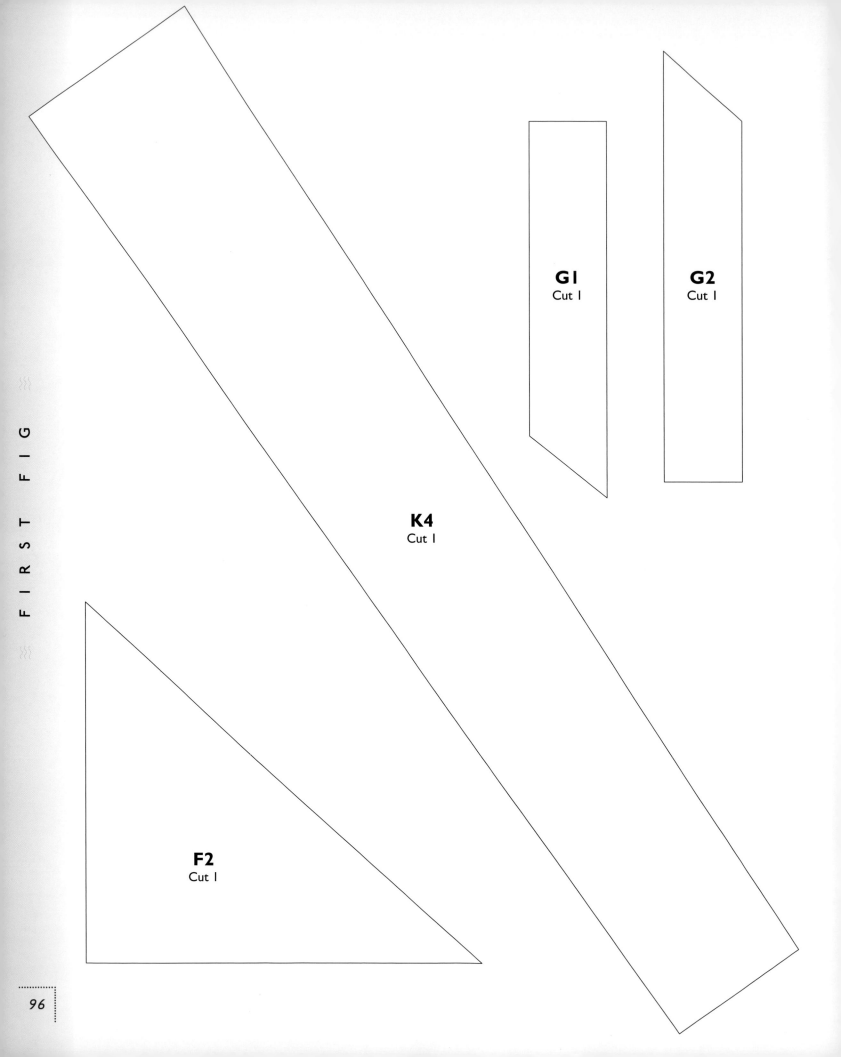

G1
Cut 1

G2
Cut 1

K4
Cut 1

F2
Cut 1

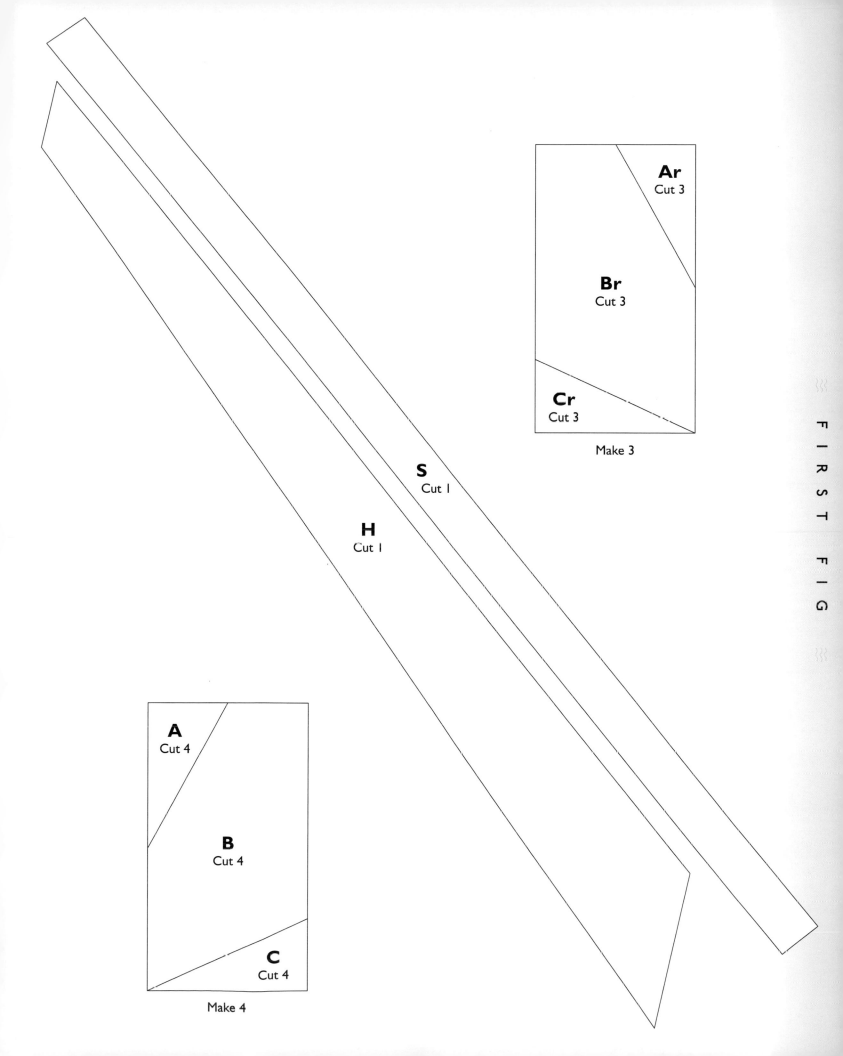

Ar
Cut 3

Br
Cut 3

Cr
Cut 3

Make 3

S
Cut 1

H
Cut 1

A
Cut 4

B
Cut 4

C
Cut 4

Make 4

Naomi Nye

It is difficult to know what to do with so much happiness.

With sadness there is something to rub up against,

a wound to tend with lotion and cloth.

When the world falls in around you, you have pieces to

pick up,

something to hold in your hands, like ticket stubs or change.

But happiness floats.

It doesn't need you to hold it down.

It doesn't need anything.

Happiness lands on the roof of the next house, singing,

and disappears when it wants to.

You are happy either way.

Even the fact that you once lived in a peaceful tree house

and now you live over a quarry of noise and dust

cannot make you unhappy.

Everything has a life of its own,

it too could wake up filled with possibilities

of coffee cake and ripe peaches,

and love even the floor which needs to be swept,

the soiled linens and scratched records...

Since there is no place large enough

to contain so much happiness,

you shrug, you raise your hands, and it flows out of you

into everything you touch. You are not responsible.

You take no credit, as the sky takes no credit

for the moon, but continues to hold it, and share it,

and in that way, be known.

Naomi Shihab Nye
1952-

Naomi Nye, a native of St. Louis, was born to a Palestinian father and an American mother. Her award-winning poetry often reflects the tension between differing cultures. Nye's work is tender and tough, sweet and biting, rich and spare. She is an accomplished children's author and has published several short stories.

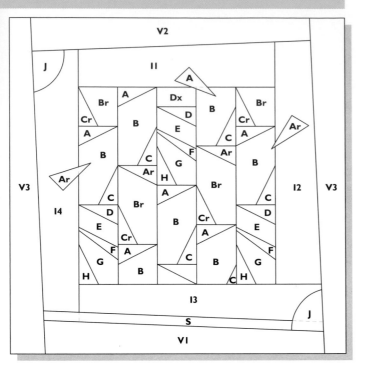

Finished block size: 14″ x 14″

Techniques: piecing, appliqué

Fabrics

Fat quarters (18″ x 22″)

• dark fabric for all large pieces (background)

Scraps:

• bright colors for the smaller triangles (we used five different fabrics)

Directions

• Piece center block: 5 A/B/C blocks, 3 D/E/F/G/H blocks, 2 Ar/Br/Cr blocks, 3 partial Ar/Br/Cr blocks, 4 Cr/Dr blocks. Assemble as shown: stitch. (Note: the paper piecing instructions in the front of the book use the D/E/F/G/H block as an example.)

• Attach inner borders in this order: I1, I2, I3, I4.

• Add accent strip. A pattern piece is provided if you would like to piece or appliqué this piece on. You can also try this: cut strip 1″ wide. Cut S 11″ long. Fold in half lengthwise, right sides out. Press. Position in place on right side of matching border piece I3, with cut edges together. Glue in place.

• Add borders in this order V1, V2, then V3s.

• Appliqué J pieces in corners and triangles in inner borders.

Tips:

Use paper piecing for this block. We used one background fabric for the largest pieces of the blocks, then added bright colors for the smaller pieces.

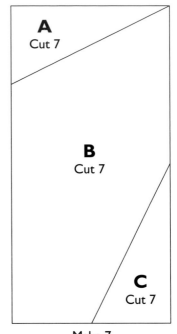

A Cut 7

B Cut 7

C Cut 7

Make 7

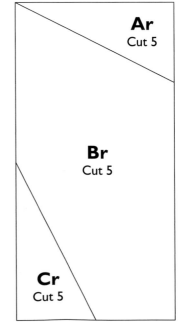

Ar Cut 5

Br Cut 5

Cr Cut 5

Make 5

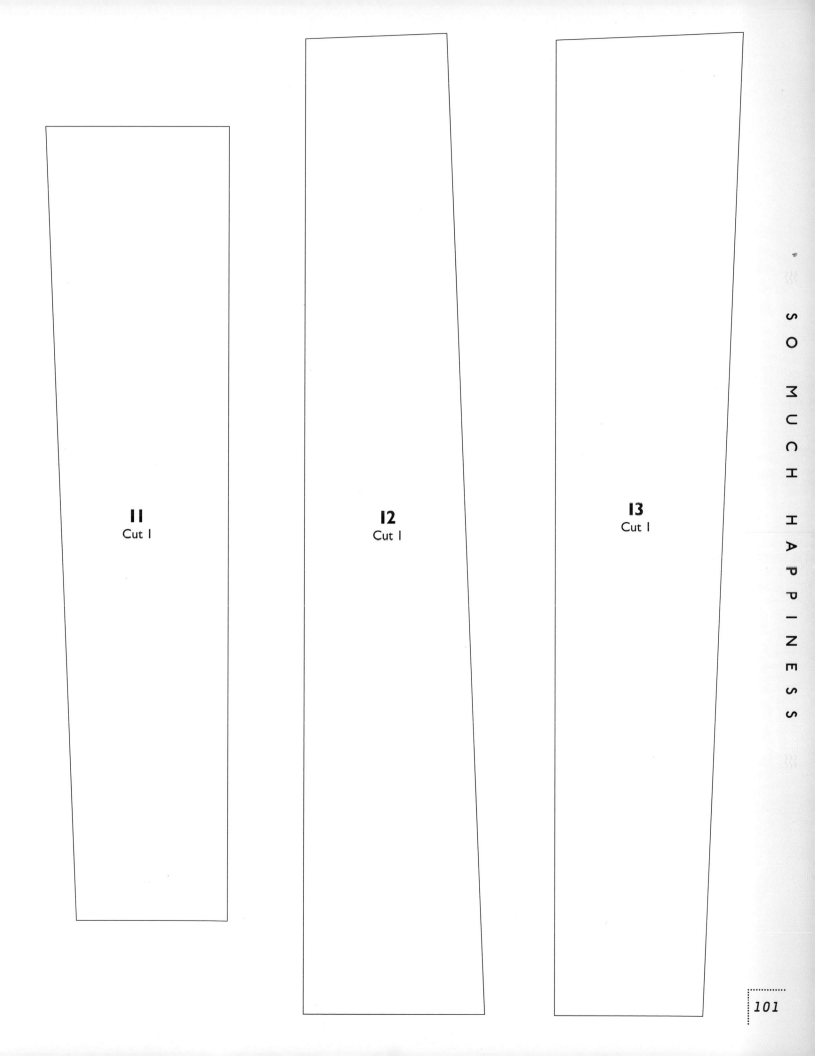

11
Cut 1

12
Cut 1

13
Cut 1

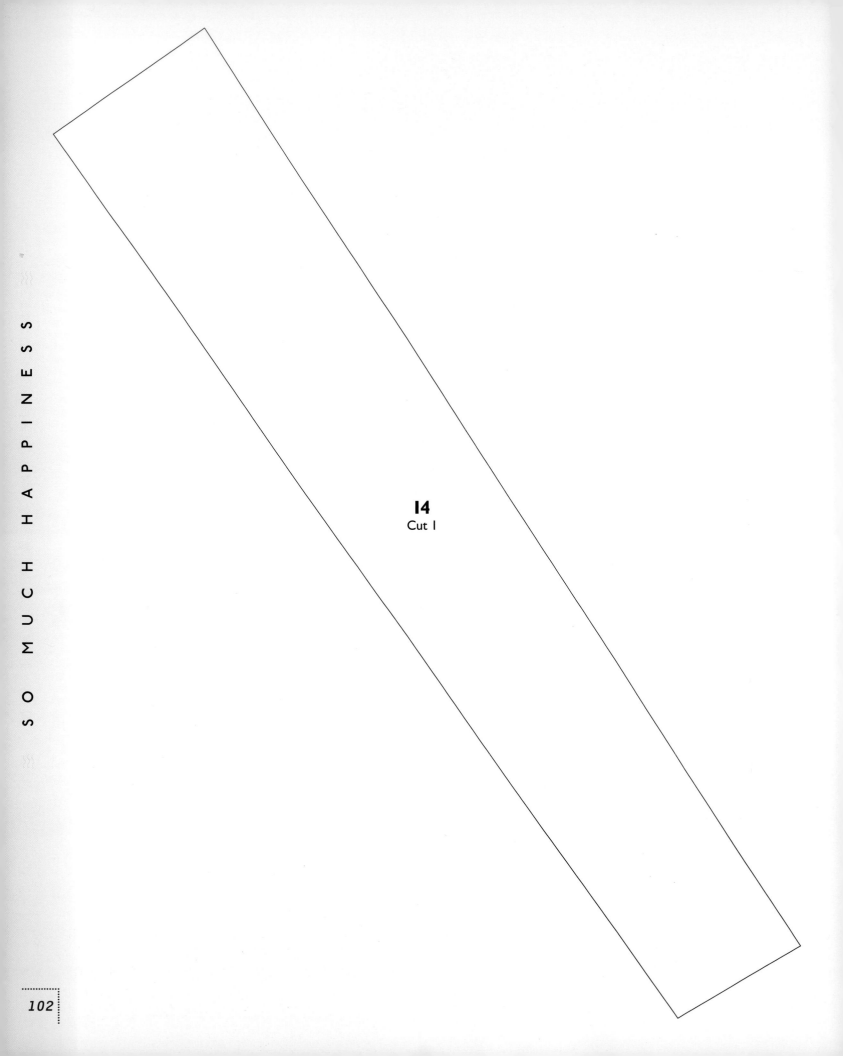

14
Cut 1

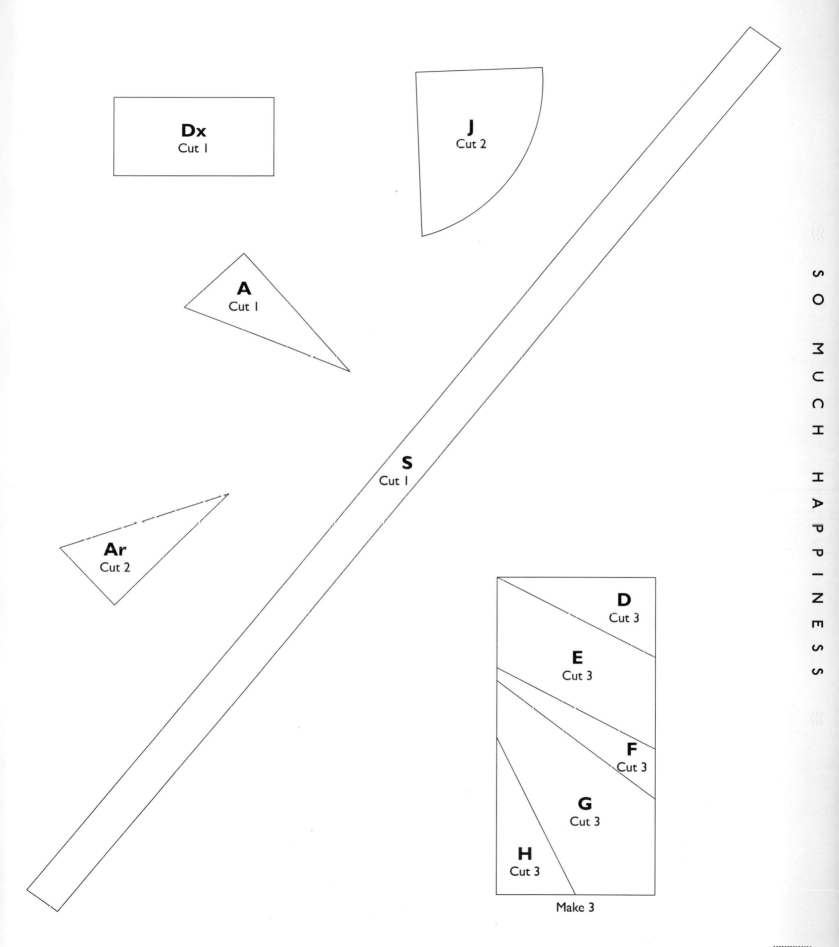

Dx
Cut 1

J
Cut 2

A
Cut 1

S
Cut 1

Ar
Cut 2

D
Cut 3

E
Cut 3

F
Cut 3

G
Cut 3

H
Cut 3

Make 3

A
Cut I

b

a

To create full-size
pattern, cut out
pattern pieces on
this page and the
following pages
and tape together
as indicated
to the right.

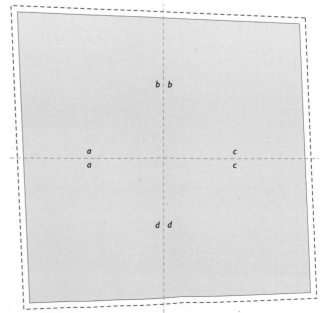

b *b*

a   *c*
a   *c*

d *d*

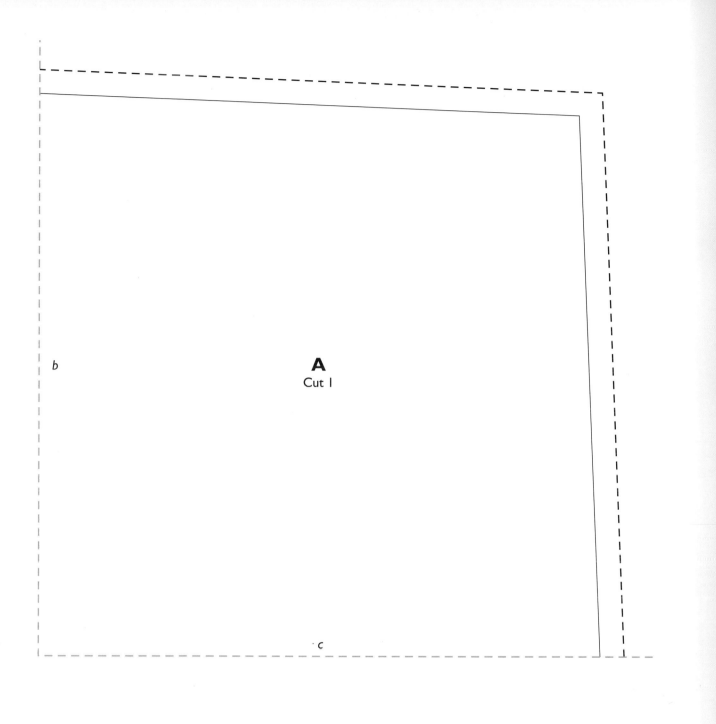

A
Cut 1

b

c

For many blocks in this book, a large background piece is used, along with four slanted border pieces. These pieces are shown on the following pages. They are labeled the same for all blocks—background A and borders V1, V2, and V3 (2). Two blocks use these same borders and background upside down to make the borders slant in a different direction. This is another design option for every block.

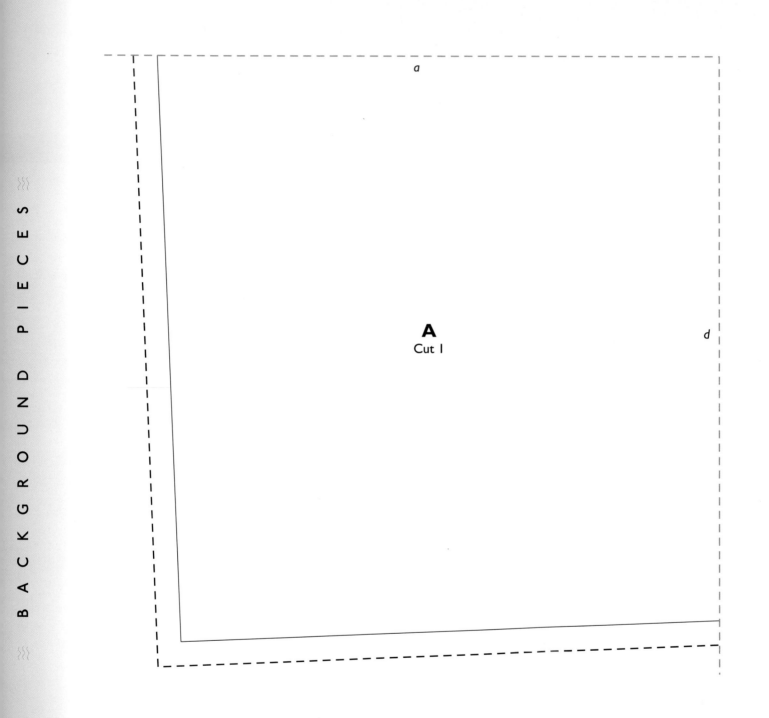

A
Cut 1

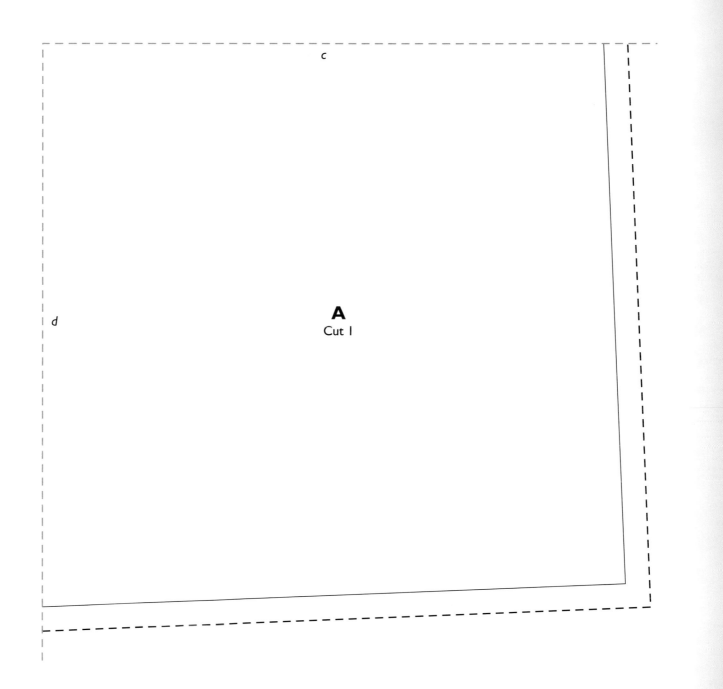

c

d

A
Cut 1

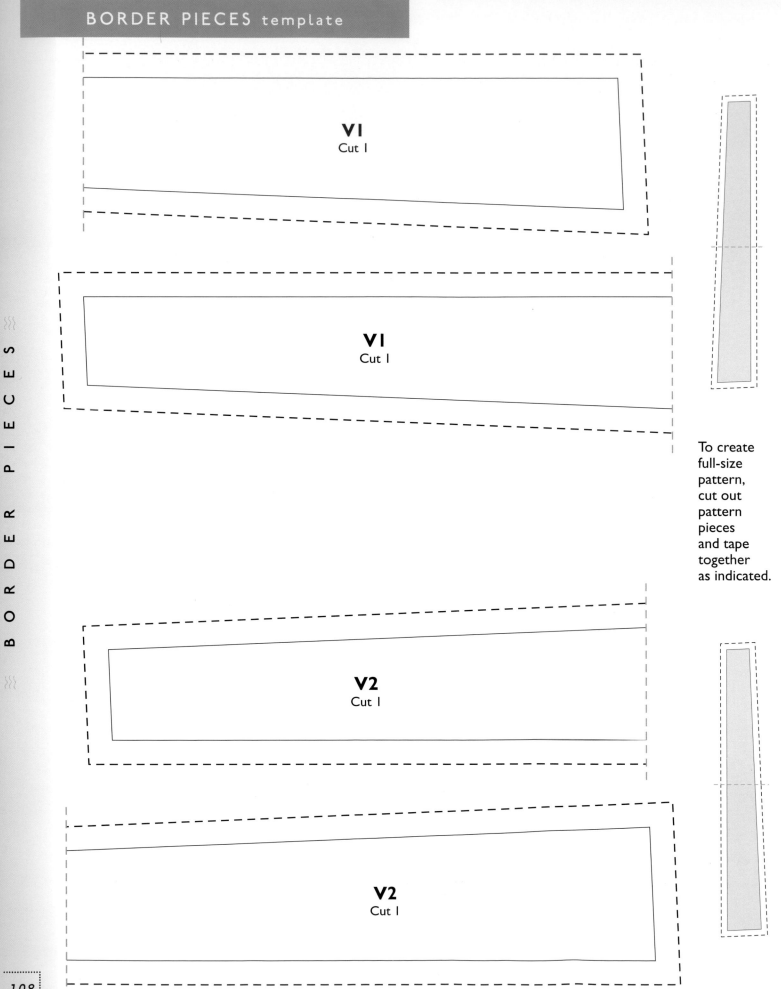

V1
Cut 1

V1
Cut 1

To create
full-size
pattern,
cut out
pattern
pieces
and tape
together
as indicated.

V2
Cut 1

V2
Cut 1

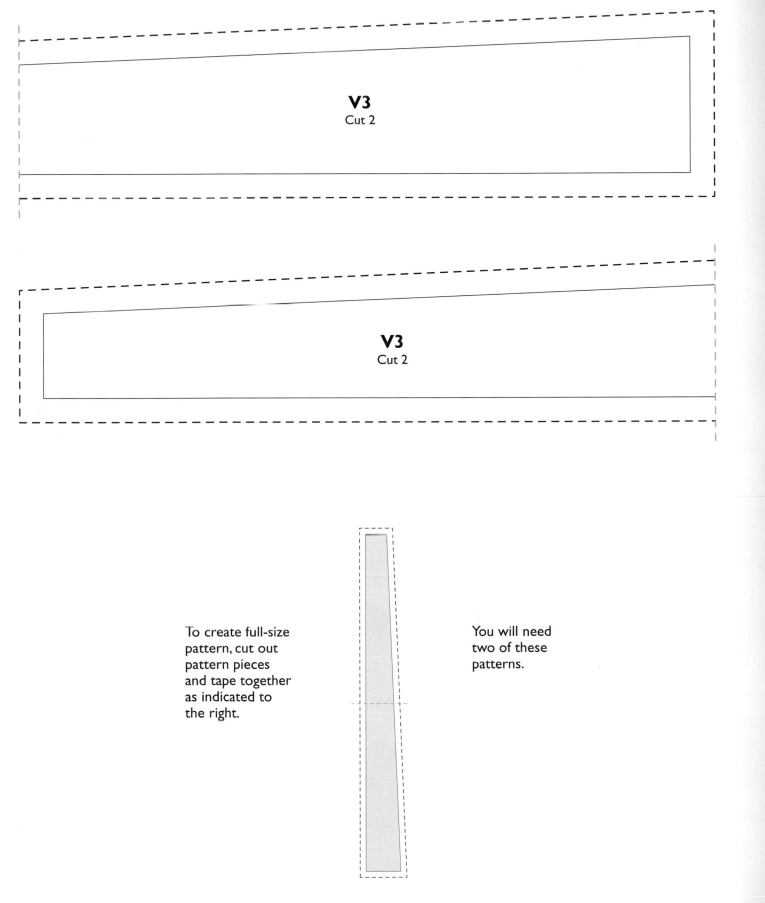

V3
Cut 2

V3
Cut 2

To create full-size pattern, cut out pattern pieces and tape together as indicated to the right.

You will need two of these patterns.

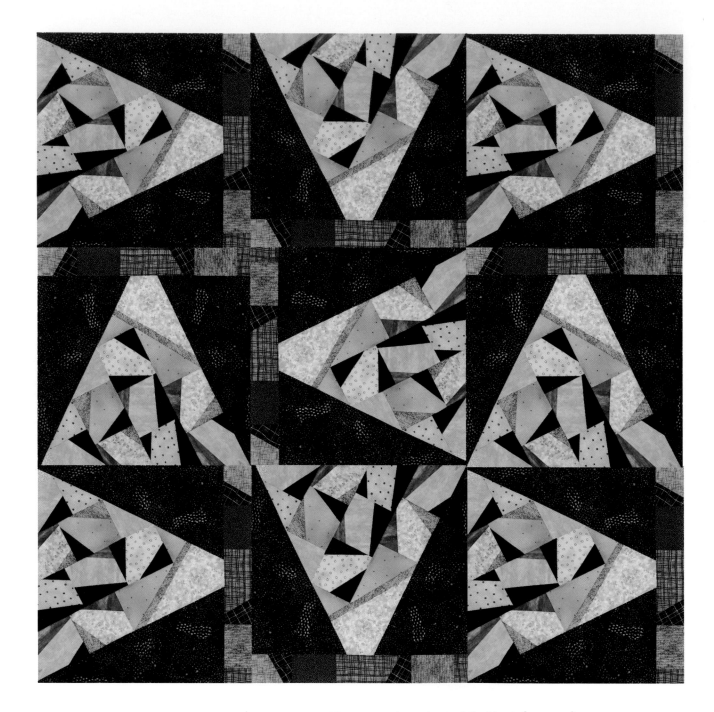

We arranged our Second fig block (page 74) to give you ideas about all of the ways you could set this block in your own quilt.

Castle Builders (page 68) offers lots of design possibilities. Imagine all the colors you could work into this quilt.

More Ideas

- Single blocks will make great mini quilts.
- Single blocks will also make interesting pillows.
- Look at the blocks and apply your own colors. We're ready to make the Feast block in a grouping of four blocks: all different colors.
- Make wall hanging of the blocks in different arrangements:
  - in vertical panels of two or three blocks (as shown).
  - in a square grouping of four blocks.
  - grouping six blocks together is another possibility.
- Borders. There are endless border options you can choose. We want to repeat shapes from the patterns in the borders—either enlarged or smaller than their original size.
- Combine the final four blocks in the book for a wall hanging. The designs in the corners of those blocks are optional. Use one for all four blocks, or use none, or combine them in a design of your choosing. You can also vary the use of the accent strips as you desire.

We liked the way these four blocks went together:
There are so many possibilities for groupings from the book's blocks.

Dreams, page 44, Caged Bird, page 50, and Dream Variations, page 56 were designed to work together. We have stitched them into a vertical panel: you could arrange them horizontally too.

CREDITS

"The Red Wheelbarrow" and "This is Just to Say" by William Carlos Williams, from COLLECTED POEMS: 1909-1939, VOLUME I, copyright © 1938 by New Directions Publishing Corp. Reprinted by permission of New Directions Publishing Corp. SALES TERRITORY: U.S./Canadian rights only.

"First Fig," "Second Fig," and "Feast" by Edna St. Vincent Millay. From Collected Poems, Harper Collins. Copyright © 1922, 1923, 1950, 1951 by Edna St. Vincent Millay and Norma Millay Ellis. All rights reserved. Reprinted by permission of Elizabeth Barnett, literary executor.

"The Road Not Taken," "Dust of Snow," and "Stopping by Woods on a Snowy Evening" from THE POETRY OF ROBERT FROST edited by Edward Connery Latham. Copyright 1923, © 1969 by Henry Holt and Co., copyright 1944, 1951 by Robert Frost. Reprinted by permission of Henry Holt and Company, LLC.

"Caged Bird", copyright © 1983 by Maya Angelou, from SHAKER, WHY DON'T YOU SING? By Maya Angelou. Used by permission of Random House.

"Dreams" and "Dream Variations" by Langston Hughes. From THE COLLECTED POEMS OF LANGSTON HUGHES by Langston Hughes. Used by permission of Alfred A. Knopf, a division of Random House, Inc.

254 " 'Hope' is the thing with feathers" by Emily Dickinson. Reprinted by permission of the publishers and the Trustees of Amherst College from THE POEMS OF EMILY DICKINSON, Thomas H. Johnson, ed., Cambridge, Mass.: The Belknap Press of Harvard University Press, Copyright © 1951, 1955, 1979 by the President and Fellows of Harvard College.

"So Much Happiness" copyright © 1982 by Naomi Shihab Nye. Reprinted by permission of Naomi Shihab Nye.